AWS Databases for AI/ML Architecting Intelligent Data Workflows

Introduction

In a cloud-native world driven by real-time intelligence, machine learning is no longer a bonus—it's a necessity. But without a solid data foundation, even the most powerful models will fail.

That's where this book comes in.

AWS Databases for AI/ML: Architecting Intelligent Data Workflows is not just another tour of AWS services. It's a practical guide to:

- Choosing the right database for your ML use case
- Streaming, storing, and structuring data for modern AI systems
- Integrating vector search, real-time inference, and multi-modal architectures

I wrote this book for architects, ML engineers, backend developers, and anyone building intelligent systems on AWS. Whether you're working with **Aurora**, **DocumentDB**, **Neptune**, **MemoryDB**, or **OpenSearch**, you'll find real-world blueprints, ready-to-run examples, and opinionated strategies.

Each chapter is designed to be **standalone and actionable**. Don't feel pressured to read it front-to-back—go where your current challenge takes you.

If you've ever found yourself asking:

- "Should I use OpenSearch or MemoryDB for vector search?"
- "How do I connect SageMaker to my data securely?"
- "Is it better to batch or stream features?"

…this book is for you.

Thank you for reading—and welcome to the future of database-driven AI.

Contents

5

Part I – Foundations of AI/ML Data Workflows on AWS

Chapter 1: Introduction to AI/ML on AWS

Artificial Intelligence (AI) and Machine Learning (ML) have evolved from academic research topics into foundational technologies driving innovation across nearly every industry. From fraud detection in finance to personalized recommendations in e-commerce and predictive maintenance in manufacturing, the possibilities are vast. AWS provides a mature, scalable, and flexible ecosystem to support every stage of the AI/ML lifecycle—particularly when it comes to data management.

This book focuses on the pivotal role of **databases** in enabling AI/ML workflows on AWS. While model training and inference are often the most visible aspects of ML, success hinges on robust, performant, and scalable **data pipelines**—and that's where AWS database services come in.

Why Databases Matter in AI/ML Workflows

Machine learning is fundamentally data-driven. Every ML model depends on high-quality, well-structured, and frequently updated data. The underlying databases that store and deliver this data must meet the unique demands of:

- **Real-time data ingestion** for online inference

- **Large-scale feature extraction** during model training

- **Low-latency querying** for user-facing recommendations or predictions

- **Streaming change data capture (CDC)** for event-driven architectures

- **Semantic search and vector similarity** for LLMs and embedding models

AWS provides multiple managed database solutions that map directly to these needs—each with its own strengths depending on the data format, access patterns, and use cases.

Key Database Services Used in AI/ML Architectures

This book explores how the following AWS-managed databases support AI/ML projects:

- **Amazon Aurora** – Fully managed relational database with native ML integration, performance insights, and zero-ETL analytics.

- **Amazon DocumentDB** – JSON-based document database, supporting vector search, schema validation, and integration with SageMaker Canvas.

- **Amazon Neptune** – Graph database ideal for recommendation systems, fraud detection, and knowledge graph modeling.

- **Amazon MemoryDB** – In-memory key-value store with vector search capabilities, useful for semantic caching and RAG (retrieval-augmented generation).

- **Amazon OpenSearch Service** – Search and analytics engine with k-NN, semantic search, anomaly detection, and ML model integration (SageMaker, Bedrock).

These databases are not just storage layers—they're **data engines** that power everything from data preprocessing and feature engineering to inference and monitoring.

AWS AI/ML Stack: The Broader Context

To understand how databases fit into the larger picture, here's a high-level view of the AWS AI/ML stack:

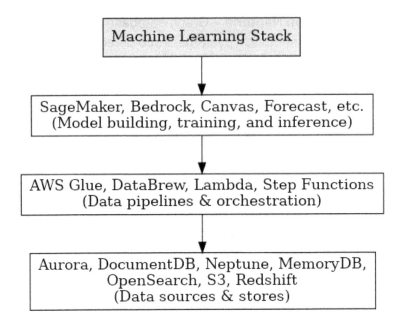

Each layer builds upon the other, and this book zooms in on how databases at the bottom layer support and enable everything above.

Core Patterns You'll Learn

Throughout the chapters, you'll discover how to:

- Query ML models directly from SQL using Amazon Aurora Machine Learning

- Stream data from DocumentDB or Aurora into ML pipelines with zero-ETL architectures

- Perform graph-based feature engineering in Amazon Neptune

- Use MemoryDB for fast vector lookups in semantic applications

- Integrate SageMaker models with OpenSearch for hybrid search and anomaly detection

- Build secure, scalable, real-time AI workflows using IAM, RDS Proxy, and Serverless

These patterns aren't hypothetical—they're drawn from real-world architectures used by companies running production-grade AI/ML systems on AWS.

Who This Book Is For

This book is designed for:

- **Machine Learning Engineers** who want to understand and optimize their data sources

- **Solution Architects** designing scalable AI workloads on AWS

- **Backend Developers** who need to integrate databases with ML inference systems

- **Data Engineers** building and maintaining ML-ready pipelines

Whether you're building real-time recommendation engines or offline batch training jobs, you'll learn how to harness the full power of AWS-managed databases to support your AI/ML needs.

Ready? Let's dive into the first service—Amazon Aurora—and see how it transforms traditional relational databases into intelligent AI enablers.

Chapter 2: Choosing the Right AWS Database for Your ML Workload

When architecting an AI/ML solution on AWS, one of the most critical design decisions you'll face is selecting the right database for your data workflows. The AWS ecosystem offers a wide variety of managed databases— each optimized for different use cases, data structures, and access patterns.

This chapter helps you navigate those options by aligning your machine learning workload requirements with the strengths of each AWS database service. Whether you're building a fraud detection model, powering a recommendation engine, or enabling a real-time chatbot with vector search, the right choice of database can make or break the performance and scalability of your system.

Key Factors to Consider

Before diving into individual services, let's explore the dimensions that matter most when selecting a database for AI/ML:

- **Data format**: Structured (relational), semi-structured (JSON), or unstructured (text, images, embeddings)

- **Access pattern**: Batch, real-time, streaming, or hybrid

- **Latency requirements**: Sub-millisecond, low-latency, or eventual consistency

- **Integration needs**: SageMaker, Redshift, Bedrock, Lambda, etc.

- **Search and retrieval style**: Key-value, vector, semantic, full-text, or graph traversal

- **Scalability and elasticity**: Autoscaling or manual provisioning

- **Security and compliance**: IAM, encryption, VPC support, etc.

Matching AWS Databases to AI/ML Use Cases

Below is a practical overview of each major AWS database and how it fits specific ML workloads.

Amazon Aurora (Relational + SQL-based ML Inference)

Best for:

- Structured tabular data

- Applications needing SQL-based model inference (via SageMaker or Comprehend)

- Feature stores and historical model training data

Highlights:

- Invoke ML models directly from SQL

- Export data to S3 for training

- Zero-ETL integration with Amazon Redshift

- Performance Insights for tuning feature queries

Amazon DocumentDB (JSON + Vector + Change Streams)

Best for:

- Semi-structured data (user profiles, events, logs)

- ML use cases needing flexible schemas

- Vector similarity search (embeddings)

Highlights:

- Vector search support

- Change streams for real-time ingestion

- Aggregation pipelines for feature transformation

- SageMaker Canvas integration for no-code modeling

15

Amazon Neptune (Graph-Based ML)

Best for:

- Relationship-heavy data

- Graph-based feature engineering

- Recommendation systems, fraud detection, knowledge graphs

Highlights:

- Gremlin and openCypher support

- Graph metrics like centrality, community detection

- Integration with SageMaker and Jupyter notebooks

Amazon MemoryDB (In-Memory Vector Store)

Best for:

- Real-time inference (RAG, semantic cache, personalization)

- Embedding similarity with low latency

- Durable in-memory storage for live models

Highlights:

- Built-in vector indexing

- RAG architecture support

- Compatible with Redis and RediSearch syntax

- Secure, durable, and scalable

Amazon OpenSearch (Search + Vector + Anomaly Detection)

Best for:

- Semantic search

- NLP applications

- Real-time anomaly detection and analytics

Highlights:

- k-NN and semantic vector search

- Integration with SageMaker and Bedrock

- Learning-to-Rank (LTR) for AI-powered search

- Full-text and structured querying (SQL, PPL)

Decision Matrix

Here's a quick comparison of common AI/ML tasks and the best-fit database:

ML Task	Best-Fit AWS Database
Fraud Detection	Aurora, Neptune
Recommendation Systems	Neptune, OpenSearch
Real-Time Inference (RAG)	MemoryDB, OpenSearch
Semantic Search	OpenSearch, MemoryDB
Graph Feature Engineering	Neptune
Personalized Experiences	DocumentDB, MemoryDB
NLP Pipelines (Search + Context)	OpenSearch, DocumentDB
Model Training from Historical DB	Aurora, DocumentDB
Real-Time Data Streams for ML	Aurora (Activity Streams), DocumentDB (Change Streams)

Hybrid Patterns

In many real-world cases, a **combination** of databases is the optimal approach. For example:

- Use **Aurora** for transactional data + **OpenSearch** for semantic search

- Use **DocumentDB** for user metadata + **MemoryDB** for real-time embedding lookup

- Use **Neptune** to extract graph features → send to SageMaker for training

AWS Glue, Lambda, and Step Functions are often used to coordinate these hybrid pipelines.

Closing Thoughts

Choosing the right AWS database for your ML workload is about more than just data storage—it's about building a data engine that aligns with your model lifecycle, latency demands, and infrastructure goals.

The chapters that follow will dive deep into each of these databases and walk you through real-world ML applications using them. Whether you're designing fraud detection engines, chatbots, or product recommendations, the right database will be your foundation.

Chapter 3: Data Architecture Patterns for Machine Learning Pipelines

At the heart of every successful machine learning system lies a well-architected data pipeline. Whether you're training complex models, deploying real-time inference, or streaming predictions into user-facing apps, the data flow must be reliable, scalable, and tightly integrated with your database infrastructure.

In this chapter, we'll explore the **key data architecture patterns** used in machine learning pipelines on AWS, focusing on how they map to various AWS-managed databases and AI/ML services. You'll learn how to organize, transform, and serve data in a way that supports high-performance model development and deployment.

The Machine Learning Data Lifecycle

Before diving into patterns, it's useful to break down the machine learning lifecycle into **data-centric phases**:

1. **Data Ingestion** – Collecting raw data from transactional systems, logs, sensors, etc.

2. **Data Storage** – Persisting structured, semi-structured, or unstructured data

3. **Feature Engineering** – Transforming raw data into meaningful features

4. **Model Training** – Using training-ready datasets to build ML models

5. **Model Inference** – Making predictions on live or batch data

6. **Monitoring & Feedback** – Logging predictions, performance metrics, and retraining triggers

Each phase demands specific architecture choices depending on performance, volume, and latency requirements.

Pattern 1: Batch-Oriented Feature Pipelines

Use Case: Offline model training with periodic updates

Architecture:

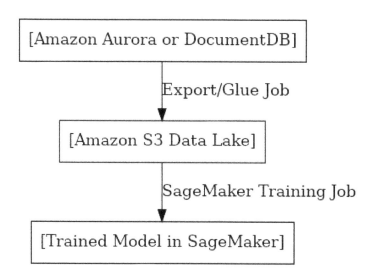

This pattern is ideal for:

- Historical training

- Customer segmentation

- Predictive modeling with daily/weekly refresh

Databases like **Aurora** and **DocumentDB** serve as the primary source of truth. AWS Glue or Lambda jobs export the data to S3, where it becomes input for SageMaker model training.

Pattern 2: Real-Time Inference with Vector Search

Use Case: Recommendations, semantic search, chatbots

Architecture:

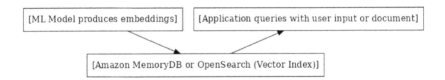

This architecture supports:

- Retrieval-Augmented Generation (RAG)

- Personalized content

- Low-latency ranking

MemoryDB offers in-memory vector search with Redis commands, while **OpenSearch** provides vector indexing with k-NN or ANN algorithms.

Pattern 3: Event-Driven ML Inference

Use Case: Fraud detection, anomaly alerting, behavioral scoring

Architecture:

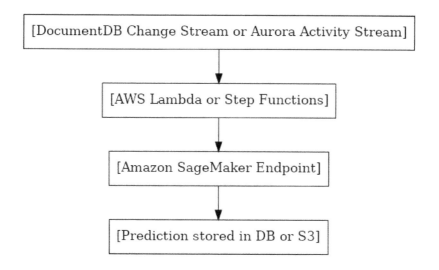

This pattern allows:

- Serverless ML inference

- Low-latency processing of new data events

- Scalable anomaly detection

You can detect document inserts/updates in real time and immediately trigger predictions via SageMaker endpoints.

Pattern 4: Graph-Enhanced Feature Engineering

Use Case: User behavior modeling, threat detection, recommendation systems

Architecture:

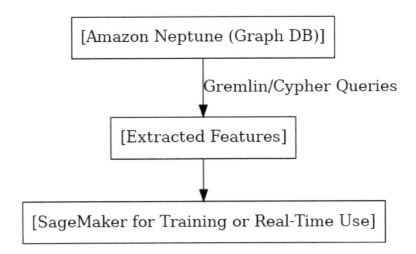

With **Amazon Neptune**, you can compute:

- Node centrality

- Path similarity

- Community detection Then feed those features into an ML pipeline.

This is especially useful in domains like finance (fraud rings), social media (influence scoring), or cybersecurity (threat propagation).

Pattern 5: Zero-ETL Real-Time Analytics

Use Case: Near-real-time dashboards, live feature extraction

Architecture:

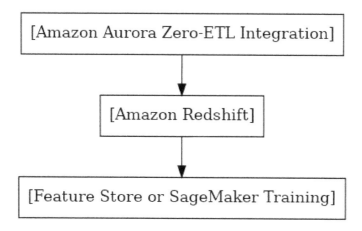

This pattern reduces latency by eliminating ETL jobs. It's ideal when:

- Data freshness matters

- You want SQL analytics + model training without delay

Pattern 6: Multi-Model Hybrid Architecture

Use Case: Systems that combine relational, search, vector, and graph data

Architecture:

```
┌─────────────────────────────────────┐
│          [Neptune]                   │
│     Relationship analysis            │
└─────────────────────────────────────┘

┌─────────────────────────────────────┐
│     [MemoryDB/OpenSearch]            │
│     Embedding-based retrieval        │
└─────────────────────────────────────┘

┌─────────────────────────────────────┐
│          [DocumentDB]                │
│     Semi-structured metadata         │
└─────────────────────────────────────┘

┌─────────────────────────────────────┐
│        [Amazon Aurora]               │
│   Structured transactions & joins    │
└─────────────────────────────────────┘
```

This pattern supports large-scale AI/ML platforms with diverse data types and access styles.

Data synchronization between services is achieved using:

- AWS Glue

- Lambda

- EventBridge

- Step Functions

Key Considerations in ML Data Architecture

- **Data freshness:** How quickly does data need to be available to models?

- **Storage format:** Use Parquet or ORC for optimized S3 storage; JSON for flexible NoSQL queries

- **Latency:** Use in-memory or pre-computed embeddings for sub-ms inference

- **Security:** Apply IAM roles, encryption, and VPC configurations per service

- **Cost:** Balance frequent queries (MemoryDB) with archival (S3)

Conclusion

The right data architecture pattern depends on your ML lifecycle stage, data velocity, and business goals. AWS offers modular, scalable components that allow you to mix and match databases, pipelines, and ML services for maximum flexibility.

In the following chapters, we'll begin a deep dive into individual databases, starting with **Amazon Aurora**, and show how each can be embedded directly into your AI/ML workflows.

Part II – Relational Databases for ML

Chapter 4: Using Aurora Machine Learning with SageMaker and Comprehend

Amazon Aurora Machine Learning (Aurora ML) integrates seamlessly with AWS AI services like Amazon SageMaker and Amazon Comprehend, enabling developers and data engineers to run real-time ML inference directly inside their SQL queries—without moving data. This chapter provides a comprehensive, implementation-ready guide for leveraging Aurora ML within intelligent AI/ML workflows.

Overview: Aurora ML in AI/ML Workflows

Aurora ML allows SQL-based applications to invoke ML models hosted in Amazon SageMaker or utilize pre-built models in Amazon Comprehend with minimal configuration. This tight integration reduces data movement latency and complexity, supporting use cases such as:

- Sentiment analysis on customer feedback

- Real-time fraud detection in transactions

- Personalization in web applications

- Document classification and entity extraction

Aurora ML supports **Aurora MySQL** and **Aurora PostgreSQL**, with slightly different capabilities and syntax.

How Aurora ML Works

Aurora ML uses a *built-in function call* mechanism to send data from Aurora SQL to SageMaker or Comprehend, get a prediction, and return the result inline in the SQL result set. The architecture consists of:

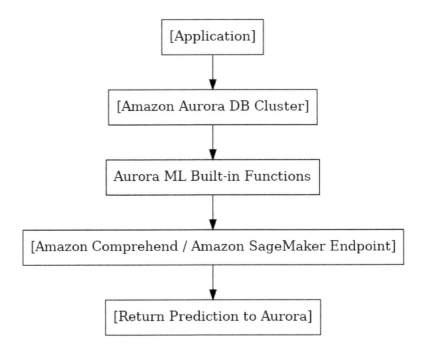

Aurora handles the invocation, security (via IAM roles), and data serialization under the hood.

Key Components

1. Aurora Integration with Amazon Comprehend

Amazon Comprehend is used for NLP tasks like sentiment analysis, entity recognition, and key phrase extraction.

Supported Aurora SQL Functions

Function	Description
`aws_comprehend_detect_sentiment( text, language)`	Returns sentiment and confidence
`aws_comprehend_detect_entities(t ext, language)`	Returns entities and types
`aws_comprehend_detect_key_phrase s(text, language)`	Extracts key phrases from the input text

Example Use Case: Sentiment Analysis
```
SELECT
    customer_id,
    feedback,
```

```
aws_comprehend_detect_sentiment(feedback,
'en') AS sentiment_result
FROM customer_feedback;
```

Output Example:

customer_id	feedback	sentiment_result
101	"Love the product!"	POSITIVE
102	"Service was too slow."	NEGATIVE

⚠ Best practice: limit text input to ≤ 5KB to avoid API errors from Comprehend.

---

2. Aurora Integration with Amazon SageMaker

Use SageMaker for custom model inference such as churn prediction, credit scoring, and classification.

Prerequisites

- Trained and deployed SageMaker endpoint.

- IAM role with SageMakerInvokeEndpoint permission.

- Endpoint must be of type `RealTimeInference`.

Aurora Function Call (Aurora PostgreSQL):

```
SELECT aws_sagemaker_invoke_endpoint(
    'churn-predictor-endpoint',
    '{"features": [0.25, 0.8, 3.0]}'
) AS prediction;
```

Aurora Function Call (Aurora MySQL):

```
SELECT aws_sagemaker_invoke_endpoint(
    'churn-predictor-endpoint',
    '[0.25, 0.8, 3.0]'
) AS prediction;
```

JSON payload format depends on your model's input signature. Test with SageMaker first.

Real-World Implementation Scenario

Use Case: Customer Churn Prediction and Sentiment Monitoring

Architecture:

33

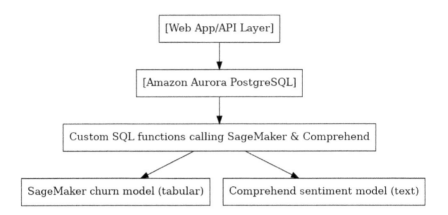

Workflow:

1. Customer leaves feedback via a form.

2. Aurora captures it into a `customer_feedback` table.

3. Trigger stored procedure to:

   ○ Analyze sentiment (Comprehend)

   ○ Invoke churn prediction (SageMaker)

4. Store results in `ml_insights` table.

5. Application adapts messaging strategy based on result.

Stored Procedure Example (PostgreSQL):

```
CREATE OR REPLACE PROCEDURE
analyze_customer_feedback()
LANGUAGE plpgsql
AS $$
BEGIN
  INSERT INTO ml_insights (customer_id,
sentiment, churn_score)
  SELECT
    f.customer_id,

aws_comprehend_detect_sentiment(f.feedback
, 'en'),
    aws_sagemaker_invoke_endpoint('churn-
model-endpoint',
        format('{"features": [%s]}',
f.feature_vector))
  FROM customer_feedback f
  WHERE NOT EXISTS (
    SELECT 1 FROM ml_insights m WHERE
m.customer_id = f.customer_id
  );
END;
$$;
```

Use Aurora's event scheduler or application
triggers to automate execution.

Security & Access Configuration

- Assign an **IAM role** to your Aurora cluster with `AmazonSageMakerFullAccess` and `ComprehendFullAccess` or scoped permissions.

- Enable **IAM DB authentication** if securing by user context.

- Attach role using `aws rds add-role-to-db-instance`.

```
aws rds add-role-to-db-instance \
    --db-instance-identifier mydbinstance \
    --feature-name SAGEMAKER \
    --role-arn
arn:aws:iam::123456789012:role/AuroraMLRol
e
```

Monitoring and Logging

- **Aurora MySQL**: Use the `mysql.general_log` or `performance_schema`.

- **Aurora PostgreSQL**: Log inference activity via `pg_stat_statements` or custom logs.

- Enable **CloudTrail** for auditing SageMaker and Comprehend API calls.

- **Latency optimization**: Minimize payload size; use batch endpoints for bulk scoring.

- **Security**: Use VPC endpoints for SageMaker and Comprehend to keep traffic private.

- **Failure handling**: Wrap inference calls in try-catch logic for NULL fallbacks.

- **Cost control**: Use inference endpoints with auto-scaling or invoke only when needed.

- **Model testing**: Validate endpoint inputs/outputs using SageMaker notebooks before calling from Aurora.

Limitations

Limitation	Description
Max payload	≤ 5 KB for Comprehend; SageMaker varies by model
Performance	Each function call is a network round-trip
Data types	JSON formatting required for SageMaker input

Supported engines	Aurora MySQL 5.7+, PostgreSQL 11+ with Aurora ML support

Summary

Aurora ML bridges the gap between SQL-based applications and advanced machine learning. By integrating directly with Amazon Comprehend and SageMaker, Aurora enables real-time intelligence within your database layer, simplifying architecture and boosting performance for AI-powered applications.

Use Aurora ML when:

- You want **real-time inference** with minimal code changes.

- You need **database-integrated AI logic** for personalization, fraud detection, or sentiment analysis.

- Your architecture values **low-latency inference** and **centralized control**.

In the next chapter, we'll explore how Aurora PostgreSQL can act as a **feature store** and support **online inference** in real-time ML pipelines.

Chapter 5: Real-Time Analytics with Zero-ETL and Amazon Redshift

Amazon Aurora's **Zero-ETL integration with Amazon Redshift** represents a significant advancement in building real-time analytics pipelines. Instead of relying on traditional extract-transform-load (ETL) workflows, data changes in Aurora are automatically and continuously replicated into Amazon Redshift, enabling immediate querying and analysis.

This chapter provides a hands-on, implementation-ready guide for configuring, using, and optimizing Zero-ETL between Aurora and Redshift for real-time analytics, especially in AI/ML-driven environments.

What is Zero-ETL with Aurora and Redshift?

Aurora's Zero-ETL integration enables **near real-time replication** of data from an Amazon Aurora database to an Amazon Redshift data warehouse **without manual ETL jobs**. It continuously streams changes from Aurora's transaction logs to Redshift, where data becomes available in seconds.

This is especially useful for:

- Generating dashboards on live transactional data

- Supporting ML feature engineering on fresh data

- Feeding AI models with up-to-date context

Supported Databases and Requirements

- **Source**: Amazon Aurora MySQL-Compatible Edition (v3.01+)

- **Target**: Amazon Redshift RA3 nodes or Redshift Serverless

- **Replication granularity**: Per database in an Aurora cluster

- **Region**: Must be in the same AWS Region (multi-Region not yet supported)

How It Works

The replication process uses Aurora's **change data capture (CDC)** capabilities and Aurora's **database activity stream (DAS)** to forward changes to a Redshift integration endpoint.

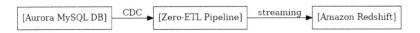

Once connected, Aurora sends inserts, updates, and deletes from the source database to Redshift tables mapped 1:1.

Setting Up Zero-ETL: Step-by-Step

1. Enable Zero-ETL Integration on Aurora

- Ensure your Aurora cluster is **MySQL v3.01.0+**

- In the AWS Console or CLI:

```
aws rds modify-db-cluster \
  --db-cluster-identifier my-aurora-
cluster \
  --enable-redshift-integration
```

2. Create a Redshift Zero-ETL Integration

- Target: An existing Redshift data warehouse

- IAM: Aurora cluster needs a role with `redshift-data:ExecuteStatement` and stream permissions

- CLI example:

```
aws redshift create-zero-etl-integration \
  --integration-name my-etl-integration \
  --source-database-arn arn:aws:rds:us-
east-1:123456789012:cluster:my-aurora-
cluster \
```

```
--target-database-name analytics \
--redshift-cluster-identifier my-
redshift-cluster \
--kms-key-id arn:aws:kms:us-east-
1:123456789012:key/my-key
```

3. Monitor Replication

- Use **CloudWatch** for lag metrics

- Use `svl_zero_etl_status` view in Redshift:

```
SELECT * FROM svl_zero_etl_status;
```

Best Practices for Real-Time Analytics Pipelines

- **Use columnar compression** in Redshift to minimize storage

- **Define primary keys** on Aurora tables to ensure proper deduplication

- **Avoid schema drift**—schema changes on Aurora won't auto-propagate

- **Partition Redshift tables** by time (e.g., daily) for query efficiency

- **Set** `binlog_format = ROW` and enable binary logging in Aurora

Example: Building a Live Customer Dashboard

Aurora table (MySQL):

```
CREATE TABLE orders (
  order_id BIGINT PRIMARY KEY,
  user_id INT,
  status VARCHAR(20),
  amount DECIMAL(10,2),
  created_at DATETIME
);
```

Redshift analytics query:

```
SELECT
  status,
  COUNT(*) AS order_count,
  SUM(amount) AS total_sales
FROM orders
WHERE created_at >= dateadd(hour, -1,
current_timestamp)
GROUP BY status;
```

This query enables your BI tools (e.g., Amazon QuickSight) to show **live KPIs** like hourly revenue, failure rates, and top customers.

- Enable **IAM authentication** for both Aurora and Redshift

- Use **VPC endpoints** to keep traffic private

- Encrypt data in transit and at rest using **AWS KMS**

- Monitor access via **AWS CloudTrail**

Limitation	Detail
Engine support	Aurora MySQL v3 only (PostgreSQL not yet supported)
Schema changes	Not automatically propagated
Region scope	Aurora and Redshift must be in the same Region
Initial sync	Requires full dump of data before real-time sync starts

Cost	Charges for Aurora activity stream and Redshift storage/compute

Using with ML/AI Workflows

This integration is ideal for AI/ML feature pipelines that need **fresh data** without running custom ETL. Example use cases:

- **SageMaker Feature Store**: Redshift can serve as a real-time feature store

- **Streaming anomaly detection**: Detect patterns in order activity or system events

- **Customer 360 models**: Train and serve models using unified, low-latency data

You can also **export Redshift data to S3** for ML model training with Athena or SageMaker Processing:

```
UNLOAD ('SELECT * FROM orders')
TO 's3://my-data-lake/orders/'
IAM_ROLE
'arn:aws:iam::123456789012:role/MyRedshift
Role'
FORMAT AS PARQUET;
```

Monitoring & Troubleshooting

- Use `svl_zero_etl_lag` and `svl_zero_etl_errors` in Redshift

- In Aurora, check logs for streaming errors

- Use **Performance Insights** to track replication overhead

Summary

Zero-ETL with Aurora and Redshift empowers teams to deliver **analytics on live operational data** with minimal engineering effort. By removing the complexity of ETL pipelines, it accelerates access to insights and powers more responsive ML applications.

Use this integration when:

- You need **real-time BI or dashboards**

- Your ML models depend on **current transactional data**

- You want to **simplify pipelines** and reduce maintenance overhead

Chapter 6: Performance Insights and Feature Extraction Optimization

Modern AI/ML pipelines increasingly rely on low-latency, high-throughput data infrastructure to support real-time inference and training. Amazon Aurora, with its integrated **Performance Insights (PI)**, provides a powerful toolset for understanding and optimizing query behavior— particularly important when databases are used for **feature extraction**, **online inference**, or **real-time scoring**.

This chapter walks you through how to use Performance Insights to detect bottlenecks, optimize feature extraction logic, and ensure your Aurora database performs well under ML-driven workloads.

What Is Performance Insights in Aurora?

Performance Insights is a **database performance monitoring and tuning tool** built into Aurora (both MySQL and PostgreSQL). It collects and visualizes detailed metrics such as **DB load**, **query execution**, **wait events**, and **active sessions**.

It helps answer questions like:

- Which queries are consuming the most CPU?

- Where are the bottlenecks in my feature transformation pipelines?

- Is my model scoring logic slowing down transactional queries?

How It Works

Performance Insights continuously samples the database and stores key performance metrics such as:

- **Average Active Sessions (AAS)**: Concurrent sessions consuming CPU or waiting

- **Top SQL statements** by resource consumption

- **Wait events** (e.g., I/O waits, locks)

- **User, host, or database** dimensions

These can be visualized in the AWS Console or queried via API.

Enabling Performance Insights

You can enable PI during or after cluster creation:

```
aws rds modify-db-cluster \
  --db-cluster-identifier my-aurora-
cluster \
  --enable-performance-insights \
```

```
--performance-insights-retention-period
7 \
   --performance-insights-kms-key-id <your-
kms-key>
```

Retention Options:

- 7 days (free tier)

- 1 to 24 months (paid)

  Performance Insights consumes minimal
  CPU. It adjusts sampling frequency during
  peak load to avoid performance impact.

Using PI to Optimize Feature Extraction Workloads

Identify Expensive Feature Queries

When Aurora is used for **real-time feature extraction**,
certain joins, aggregations, or transformations may
dominate database load.

In PI Console:

- Select "Top SQL"

- Filter by high CPU or I/O usage

- Look for slow or repetitive queries (e.g., calculating rolling aggregates)

Example query flagged:

```
SELECT user_id, COUNT(*)
FROM page_views
WHERE view_time > NOW() - INTERVAL 1 HOUR
GROUP BY user_id;
```

Optimization Strategy:

- Use **pre-aggregated materialized views** (Aurora PostgreSQL)

- Push logic to downstream systems like Redshift for batch features

- Use indexed filters and limit result sets

Analyze Wait Events in Feature Pipelines

If your features are built from complex joins or large text columns (e.g., NLP inputs), you may encounter:

- `io/file/data` → Indicates disk I/O

- `cpu` → Indicates compute-bound queries

- `lock:table metadata` → Suggests contention on DDL or schema changes

Querying the PI dimension "Wait Events" will highlight where time is lost.

SQL Analysis via Wait Events:

```
SELECT *
FROM performance_insights.query_metrics
WHERE wait_event_type = 'io/file/data';
```

Use this to decide whether to:

- Repartition large tables

- Use in-memory caching (e.g., ElastiCache)

- Introduce **read replicas** for feature pipelines

Monitor Model Scoring Latency in SQL

Aurora supports **ML scoring inside SQL** using Aurora ML with SageMaker or Comprehend. Performance Insights helps validate:

- Is the model endpoint introducing high latency?

- Are scoring queries increasing DB load?

Example monitored query:

```
SELECT user_id,
aws_sagemaker_invoke_endpoint('fraud-
endpoint', payload)
FROM transactions
WHERE created_at >= NOW() - INTERVAL 10
MINUTE;
```

Solution:

- Rate-limit inference calls via WHERE clause

- Offload bulk inference to batch jobs

- Use **connection pooling** (e.g., with RDS Proxy)

Best Practices for ML Feature Extraction and Scoring

- **Tag feature queries** using comments for easy filtering in PI:

```
SELECT /*feature_extraction*/ ...;
```

- Use **reader endpoints** for analytical workloads, isolating inference from writes

- Schedule feature queries to run during low-traffic windows

- Precompute static features and cache results

- Use **custom endpoints** to direct feature queries to specific replicas

---

Using PI APIs for Custom Dashboards

For observability in ML pipelines, you can extract PI metrics via the API:

```
aws pi get-resource-metrics \
  --service-type RDS \
  --identifier <cluster-arn> \
  --metric-queries '[{"Metric":
"db.load.avg", "GroupBy": {"Group":
"db.sql.tokenized"}}]' \
  --start-time <timestamp> \
  --end-time <timestamp>
```

This allows integration with:

- Prometheus / Grafana dashboards

- SageMaker Pipelines for adaptive feature scaling

- Lambda functions to alert when scoring overhead increases

Real-World Example: Feature Extraction Latency Reduction

A retail analytics application used Aurora PostgreSQL for building real-time customer features. Queries were scanning millions of rows per session.

After using Performance Insights:

- They identified a frequent aggregation on unindexed columns.

- Added GIN indexes and rewrote the query to use window functions.

- Reduced average query latency from **12s to 1.3s**, improving model accuracy due to fresher features.

Security and Access Control

- Performance Insights data is **encrypted using KMS**

- Fine-grained access via IAM policies (e.g., allow developers to view only specific clusters)

- Logs of PI API calls can be captured via **AWS CloudTrail**

Limitations and Considerations

Limitation	Detail
Serverless support	Aurora Serverless v2 supported (some features may vary)
Not for long-term forensics	Use CloudWatch or enhanced monitoring for longer histories
No alerting natively	Integrate with CloudWatch for proactive alerting
Pricing	Free tier includes 7 days; longer retention incurs cost

Summary

Performance Insights is an indispensable tool for AI/ML architects and engineers using Aurora for feature extraction, real-time inference, or heavy analytical queries. It bridges the gap between SQL visibility and ML performance, enabling smarter query design, proactive scaling, and robust monitoring.

Use PI when:

- You're deploying **ML scoring inside SQL**

- You need to **optimize online feature engineering**

- You want to **monitor query load trends** across ML workloads

Chapter 7: Streaming Aurora Changes for ML Pipelines with Activity Streams

Modern ML pipelines often require a continuous flow of fresh, relevant data to maintain model accuracy and responsiveness. When feature stores, data lakes, or ML inference engines depend on near-real-time data updates from your transactional databases, **streaming change data** from Amazon Aurora becomes essential.

Amazon Aurora provides **Database Activity Streams (DAS)**—a secure, low-latency, near-real-time stream of database activity. This chapter explores how to use Aurora Activity Streams to feed ML pipelines with timely and trustworthy data updates, enabling capabilities like online feature stores, model retraining triggers, and fraud detection systems.

What Are Aurora Database Activity Streams (DAS)?

Aurora Activity Streams capture and stream **low-level database activity**, including SQL statements, bind variables, user information, and execution context. This stream is:

- **Near real-time** (sub-second latency)

- **Immutable** and **cryptographically signed** (for compliance)

- **Integrated with AWS Kinesis** for delivery and processing

Unlike logical replication or CDC tools that work at the row-change level, DAS provides **full activity-level observability**. It's best suited for:

- Auditing and compliance

- Streaming ETL and data lake ingestion

- Real-time feature ingestion for ML

- Behavioral anomaly detection (e.g., fraud)

How It Works

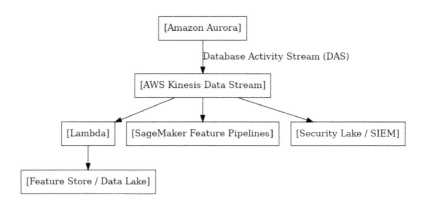

Once enabled, Aurora DAS securely pushes database activity into a Kinesis stream, which you can consume using AWS Lambda, Kinesis Data Firehose, or other analytics tools.

Enabling Aurora Activity Streams

Currently supported on:

- Aurora PostgreSQL-compatible editions (version ≥ 10.7+)

- Aurora MySQL-compatible editions (version ≥ 5.7.12)

Step 1: Create a Kinesis Data Stream

```
aws kinesis create-stream \
  --stream-name aurora-activity-stream \
  --shard-count 1
```

Step 2: Enable DAS on Aurora

Via AWS CLI:

```
aws rds start-activity-stream \
  --resource-arn arn:aws:rds:us-east-
1:123456789012:cluster:my-aurora-cluster \
  --mode sync \
  --kms-key-id arn:aws:kms:us-east-
1:123456789012:key/my-kms-key \
  --kinesis-stream-name aurora-activity-
stream
```

Modes:

- sync – delivers activities near-real time (preferred for ML pipelines)

- async – delivers with a delay (better for logging/auditing)

Using DAS for ML Feature Engineering

Real-Time Feature Pipeline Example

Use case: You want to track customer behavior across sessions to build up-to-date embeddings or fraud features.

Architecture:

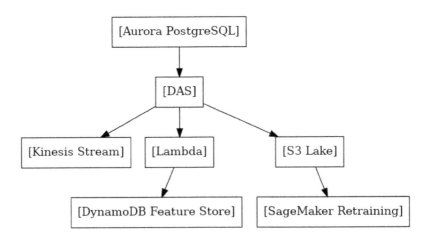

Example Lambda Consumer (Python):

```python
import base64, json

def lambda_handler(event, context):
    for record in event['Records']:
        payload =
base64.b64decode(record['kinesis']['data']
)
        activity = json.loads(payload)

        # Extract relevant fields
        user = activity['dbUser']
        sql = activity['statement']
        timestamp = activity['eventTime']

        if "INSERT INTO transactions" in
sql:

process_transaction_event(user, sql,
timestamp)
```

Use this to:

- Increment counters in Redis or DynamoDB for real-time features

- Append records to an S3 bucket for batch model training

- Enrich with external context before scoring with SageMaker

- All activity stream records are **signed and encrypted** using your **KMS key**

- **Cannot be altered or suppressed**, making it ideal for regulated workloads

- Supports **IAM fine-grained access control** over the stream

- Use **CloudTrail** to audit start/stop of activity streams

Common ML Use Cases for Aurora Activity Streams

Use Case	Integration Pattern
Real-time fraud detection	DAS → Kinesis → Lambda → SageMaker endpoint
Online feature store updates	DAS → Kinesis → Redis / DynamoDB
Model retraining triggers	DAS → S3 → SageMaker Pipelines

Personalized recommendations	DAS → Firehose → Redshift ML
Security anomaly detection	DAS → OpenSearch / Security Lake

Optimizing DAS for ML Workloads

- **Filter noise early**: Build lightweight Lambda filters to route only relevant SQL actions

- **Batch writes**: Use Kinesis aggregation to reduce S3 or DynamoDB write pressure

- **Use reader clusters**: Offload ML-driven activity to read replicas to avoid contention

- **Align schema design**: Avoid frequent DDL that clutters the activity stream

Limitations and Considerations

Limitation	Detail
Write-only	You see activity, not full row diffs (not a full CDC replacement)
Cost	Priced per Aurora cluster + Kinesis usage
Engine support	Aurora MySQL & PostgreSQL, but versions vary

Stream lag	Typically sub-second, but check CloudWatch for spike alerts

Monitoring and Troubleshooting

- Use **CloudWatch metrics** for stream throughput and lag

- Check Aurora logs for stream delivery errors

- Enable **CloudTrail** to track start/stop or access operations

- Set up **Kinesis enhanced fan-out** for multiple consumers (e.g., ML, security)

Summary

Aurora Activity Streams are a powerful tool for bridging OLTP and ML systems. By exposing near-real-time database activity through a secure, immutable channel, DAS enables ML pipelines to stay fresh, relevant, and responsive.

Use DAS when:

- You need **low-latency feature updates**

- You want **real-time observability** into behavior

- Your pipeline must **stream Aurora changes** into S3, SageMaker, or DynamoDB

Chapter 8: Exporting Aurora Data to Amazon S3 for ML Model Training

Training effective ML models requires access to high-quality, structured, and up-to-date data. When Amazon Aurora is your source of truth for transactional or event-driven data, exporting that data to Amazon S3 becomes a key part of the machine learning pipeline—enabling batch feature engineering, model training, validation, and retraining workflows.

This chapter guides you through practical, secure, and scalable methods for exporting data from Amazon Aurora (MySQL and PostgreSQL) to Amazon S3. You'll learn how to automate data exports, optimize them for ML workloads, and align export processes with SageMaker and data lake architecture.

Why Export Aurora Data to S3 for ML?

- **Model training**: Use curated Aurora data to train models in Amazon SageMaker or EMR

- **Feature pipelines**: Generate engineered features at scale with Athena, Glue, or Spark

- **Version control**: Store historical snapshots for reproducibility

- **Data lake integration**: Feed Aurora data into a unified S3-based lake for analytics and AI

S3 provides the durability, scalability, and integration points required for modern AI/ML architectures.

Methods to Export Aurora Data to S3

There are three primary methods, depending on the database engine and use case:

Method	Aurora Engine	Format	Use Case
Aurora MySQL `SELECT INTO OUTFILE S3`	MySQL	CSV, TSV, JSON	Fast exports of query results
Aurora PostgreSQL `aws_s3.export_table` **(aws_s3 extension)**	PostgreSQL	CSV	Table or query result export
Snapshot Export to S3	Both	Parquet	Full-cluster or full-table backups

Exporting from Aurora MySQL Using `SELECT INTO OUTFILE S3`

Aurora MySQL supports direct export of query results into S3 buckets.

Prerequisites:

- Aurora MySQL 5.7+ or 8.0+

- The cluster must be **in a VPC with S3 access**

- IAM role attached to Aurora with `AmazonS3FullAccess` (or scoped)

- S3 bucket with correct bucket policy for RDS

SQL Example:

```
SELECT *
FROM transactions
INTO OUTFILE S3 's3://my-ml-
datasets/transactions.csv'
FIELDS TERMINATED BY ','
LINES TERMINATED BY '\n'
OVERWRITE ON;
```

Best Practices:

- Use WHERE clauses to limit rows (e.g., date ranges)

- Export to gzip-compressed files using `FORMAT CSV GZIP`

- Export hourly/daily partitions for parallel processing in Spark/SageMaker

---

Exporting from Aurora PostgreSQL Using the aws_s3 Extension

Aurora PostgreSQL provides the aws_s3 extension to export tables or query results to S3.

Enable extension:

```
CREATE EXTENSION IF NOT EXISTS aws_s3
CASCADE;
```

SQL Example: Export a table

```
SELECT aws_s3.table_export_to_s3(
    'public.transactions',
    '',
    'us-east-1',
    'my-ml-datasets',
    'transactions_2025_03_30.csv',
    'my-aurora-export-role'
);
```

SQL Example: Export a custom query

```
SELECT aws_s3.query_export_to_s3(
  'SELECT user_id, SUM(amount) FROM
transactions GROUP BY user_id',
  '',
  'us-east-1',
  'my-ml-datasets',
  'agg_features.csv',
  'my-aurora-export-role'
);
```

Tips:

- Use parallel queries to split large data by key (e.g., user_id ranges)

- Store in partitioned folders: `s3://my-ml-datasets/date=2025-03-30/`

Snapshot Export to S3 (Full Backup)

For complete datasets or snapshot-based training pipelines, export an Aurora snapshot to S3.

Steps:

```
aws rds start-export-task \
  --export-task-identifier ml-export-
20250330 \
```

```
--source-arn arn:aws:rds:us-east-
1:123456789012:cluster-snapshot:aurora-
snap-0301 \
  --s3-bucket-name my-ml-snapshots \
  --iam-role-arn
arn:aws:iam::123456789012:role/auroraSnaps
hotExportRole \
  --kms-key-id arn:aws:kms:us-east-
1:123456789012:key/abc123
```

- Output format: **Apache Parquet**

- Granular control over **schemas and tables**

- Can be integrated with Glue Data Catalog and Athena

Use Cases:

- Historical training datasets

- Reproducibility in model experiments

- Data versioning via snapshot timestamps

Security and Access Control

- Use **IAM roles** with least privilege:

71

- o **S3**: `s3:PutObject, s3:ListBucket`

  - o **RDS**: `rds:StartExportTask, rds:DescribeExportTasks`

- Attach IAM role to DB cluster:

```
aws rds add-role-to-db-cluster \
  --db-cluster-identifier my-cluster \
  --role-arn
arn:aws:iam::123456789012:role/my-export-
role \
  --feature-name S3_EXPORT
```

- Secure bucket with **encryption (SSE-KMS)** and **block public access**

Real-World ML Use Case: Predictive Churn Modeling

Pipeline Example:

1. Daily batch job exports `user_activity` to `s3://my-datalake/user_activity/date=2025-03-30/`

2. SageMaker Processing job runs Spark-based feature generation

3. Features stored in SageMaker Feature Store

4. Trained model deployed via SageMaker endpoint

5. Aurora SQL connects to SageMaker via Aurora ML for real-time predictions

This hybrid offline/online approach balances scale and latency.

Cost Optimization Tips

- Compress CSV output: Use `.gz` suffix or compression option

- Partitioned exports reduce downstream scan costs in Athena or SageMaker

- Snapshot exports in Parquet are cheaper to scan and train with

- Export only necessary columns and filtered rows

- Monitor export status:

  - `pg_stat_activity` (PostgreSQL)

  - `SHOW PROCESSLIST` (MySQL)

  - `describe-export-tasks` (Snapshot exports)

- Use **S3 event notifications** to trigger downstream ML workflows

- Enable logging with **Aurora Enhanced Monitoring** and **CloudWatch**

Summary

Exporting data from Aurora to S3 is a critical bridge between transactional systems and ML platforms. It enables reproducible, scalable, and automated ML workflows while decoupling OLTP and batch analytics environments.

Use S3 exports when:

- You need **offline model training** or **backtesting**

- Your **ML pipelines run on SageMaker, EMR, or Glue**

- You want **Parquet-based data lake integration**

Chapter 9: Leveraging Aurora PostgreSQL ML Functions

Amazon Aurora PostgreSQL-Compatible Edition offers built-in support for invoking machine learning inference functions directly within SQL queries, enabling intelligent applications that respond to data in real-time. By integrating with AWS AI services like **Amazon Comprehend** and **Amazon SageMaker**, Aurora PostgreSQL lets developers and data engineers embed ML predictions into existing database workflows—without moving data out of the system.

This chapter details how to discover, configure, and effectively use **Aurora ML functions** in Aurora PostgreSQL to enhance feature engineering, scoring, personalization, and NLP workflows.

Why Use ML Functions in Aurora PostgreSQL?

- **No ETL required**: Perform inference on live data without exporting it.

- **Low latency**: Useful for real-time scoring or decision systems.

- **SQL-native experience**: Inference results are available inline with query results.

- **Secure and auditable**: Leverages IAM roles and encrypted communication.

Types of Aurora ML Functions

Aurora PostgreSQL supports several ML function families:

Function Group	Description	Backed By
aws_comprehend_*	Natural Language Processing (NLP) functions	Amazon Comprehend
aws_sagemaker_invoke_endpoint()	Inference from custom models	Amazon SageMaker
aurora_stat_* and aurora_*_status()	Cluster diagnostics	Aurora PostgreSQL internals

We will focus on the first two categories for ML purposes.

Using Amazon Comprehend for NLP in SQL

Aurora provides native SQL functions that wrap Comprehend's NLP models, allowing direct text analysis from within SQL queries.

Supported functions:

```
aws_comprehend_detect_sentiment(text,
language_code)
aws_comprehend_detect_entities(text,
language_code)
aws_comprehend_detect_key_phrases(text,
language_code)
```

Example – Sentiment Analysis:

```
SELECT
  user_id,
  feedback,

aws_comprehend_detect_sentiment(feedback,
'en') AS sentiment
FROM customer_feedback
WHERE created_at >= now() - INTERVAL '1
day';
```

Example – Entity Detection:

```
SELECT
  aws_comprehend_detect_entities('Amazon
launched a new region in Spain', 'en');
```

Best Practices:

- Use batching and filtering to minimize API calls.

- Keep text inputs under **5 KB** per row.

- Monitor usage to stay within service quotas.

Invoking Amazon SageMaker Endpoints from Aurora

Aurora PostgreSQL supports invoking real-time inference endpoints from SageMaker using:

```
aws_sagemaker_invoke_endpoint(endpoint_nam
e, json_payload)
```

This allows real-time ML model scoring inside SQL queries—ideal for fraud detection, churn prediction, or personalized recommendations.

Example – Real-time Inference for Churn Prediction:

```
SELECT
  customer_id,
  aws_sagemaker_invoke_endpoint(
    'churn-model-v2',
    format('{"features": [%s, %s, %s]}',
feature1, feature2, feature3)
```

```
  ) AS churn_score
FROM live_features
WHERE last_activity > now() - INTERVAL '5
minute';
```

Response Handling:

- Function returns a **text JSON string**.

- Use `jsonb_extract_path_text()` or `->>` to parse results if needed.

Example – Extracting Prediction:

```
SELECT
  (aws_sagemaker_invoke_endpoint('my-
endpoint', '{"age": 45}')::jsonb)-
>>'prediction' AS result;
```

IAM Role Configuration

For both Comprehend and SageMaker, Aurora must be granted permission via an IAM role.

Steps:

1. Create an IAM role with
   `sagemaker:InvokeEndpoint` and

`comprehend:*` **permissions.**

2. Attach the role to the Aurora cluster:

```
aws rds add-role-to-db-cluster \
  --db-cluster-identifier my-cluster \
  --role-arn
arn:aws:iam::123456789012:role/AuroraMLRol
e \
  --feature-name SAGEMAKER
```

3. Grant access within PostgreSQL:

```
GRANT EXECUTE ON FUNCTION
aws_sagemaker_invoke_endpoint TO
your_user;
```

Security & Network Setup

- Use **VPC endpoints** for SageMaker and Comprehend to keep traffic internal.

- KMS encryption is used for in-transit and at-rest data.

- Monitor usage with **CloudTrail** and **Aurora Performance Insights**.

Real-World Use Case: Real-Time Recommendation Engine

1. Aurora PostgreSQL stores customer session data.

2. A view calculates real-time behavior features.

3. SageMaker endpoint (deep learning model) is invoked to return product suggestions.

```
CREATE VIEW session_features AS
SELECT
  session_id,
  json_build_object(
    'pages_viewed', page_views,
    'cart_items', cart_count
  ) AS feature_payload
FROM session_stats;

SELECT
  session_id,

aws_sagemaker_invoke_endpoint('recommendat
ion-v1', feature_payload::text) AS
recommendations
```

```
FROM session_features;
```

This architecture powers responsive UX personalization based on live interactions.

Performance and Cost Optimization

- Use the **reader endpoint** for inference-only workloads.

- Limit concurrent inference calls via connection pooling or throttling.

- Monitor SageMaker endpoint invocation costs.

- Use **caching** for repeated predictions on the same input.

Limitations and Considerations

Limitation	Description
Max payload	≤ 5 KB (Comprehend), varies for SageMaker
Result parsing	Returns JSON as text; parsing may require extra processing

Engine versions	Supported in Aurora PostgreSQL 11+
Debugging	Errors from SageMaker or Comprehend surface as SQL errors

Discovering Available Functions

Use Aurora's built-in function browser:

```sql
SELECT * FROM aurora_list_builtins()
WHERE "Name" ILIKE '%sagemaker%' OR "Name"
ILIKE '%comprehend%';
```

This is helpful to list supported ML functions and their argument types.

Summary

Aurora PostgreSQL ML functions offer a powerful, SQL-native way to embed machine learning into applications and workflows—enabling intelligent predictions, real-time decisions, and seamless integration with AWS AI services.

Use Aurora ML functions when:

- You need **real-time scoring** without leaving the database

- You're building **ML-assisted SQL workflows** (e.g., fraud checks, recommendations)

- You want to **simplify architecture** by removing ETL steps

Chapter 10: Autoscaling ML Apps with Aurora Serverless v2

Machine learning applications can experience unpredictable spikes in database activity—whether from model inference requests, user personalization, feature extraction, or real-time monitoring. Amazon Aurora Serverless v2 provides **on-demand autoscaling of database compute capacity**, making it ideal for **ML workloads that require scalability, cost efficiency, and low-latency response**.

In this chapter, you'll learn how to architect ML applications using Aurora Serverless v2 (ASv2), including how it differs from v1, how to configure autoscaling, and how to optimize it for inference-heavy or feature-rich applications.

Why Aurora Serverless v2 for ML?

- **Granular autoscaling (0.5–128 ACUs)**: Scales up/down in fractions of a second based on load.

- **Always-on connections**: Unlike v1, there's no cold-start penalty.

- **Multi-AZ and read replica support**: For high availability and read scaling.

- **Fine-tuned for event-driven and spiky ML workloads**: Ideal for apps where model usage is unpredictable.

Aurora Serverless v2 vs v1: Key Differences

Feature	Serverless v1	Serverless v2
Scaling granularity	In steps (ACUs)	Continuous (fractions of ACUs)
Cold start delay	Yes	No (always warm)
Read replicas	Not supported	Supported
Multi-AZ support	No	Yes
Manual scaling control	No	Yes (max/min ACUs)
Production-ready	Limited	☑ Fully production-ready

Architecture for ML Inference Using Aurora Serverless v2

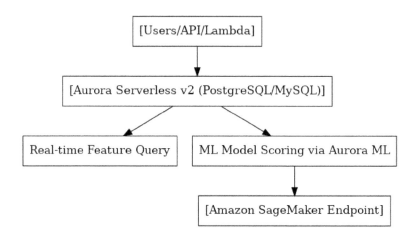

This architecture supports real-time personalization, fraud scoring, or ML-assisted search via SQL queries that interact with SageMaker and Aurora feature tables.

Creating an Aurora Serverless v2 Cluster for ML

Step 1: Create DB Cluster

Use the console or CLI:

```
aws rds create-db-cluster \
  --engine aurora-postgresql \
  --engine-version 14.6 \
  --scaling-configuration
MinCapacity=2,MaxCapacity=32,AutoPause=fal
se \
  --db-cluster-identifier ml-serverless-
cluster \
```

```
--serverless-v2-scaling-configuration
MinCapacity=2,MaxCapacity=32
```

Step 2: Create DB Instance (writer)

```
aws rds create-db-instance \
  --db-instance-identifier ml-serverless-
instance \
  --db-cluster-identifier ml-serverless-
cluster \
  --engine aurora-postgresql \
  --db-instance-class db.serverless
```

Step 3: Optional Read Replica

Add a read replica for separating ML workloads:

```
aws rds create-db-instance \
  --db-instance-identifier ml-serverless-
reader \
  --db-cluster-identifier ml-serverless-
cluster \
  --engine aurora-postgresql \
  --db-instance-class db.serverless \
  --promotion-tier 15
```

Use this instance for **read-heavy model inference queries** or feature extraction.

Aurora Serverless v2 scales based on CPU, memory, and active connections.

Typical ML Triggers:

- Burst of inference queries from a frontend app

- Feature retrieval for batch scoring or model retraining

- Deep joins or aggregates on live data

Monitoring Scaling:

Use **CloudWatch metrics**:

- ServerlessDatabaseCapacity

- ACUsConsumed

- DatabaseConnections

- AuroraReplicaLag (for read scaling)

Set alarms to trigger if max capacity is consistently hit—indicating under-provisioned configuration.

An ecommerce personalization service runs a Python API that:

1. Fetches user interaction history from Aurora (ASv2)

2. Uses that data to invoke a SageMaker model

3. Renders recommendations

At low traffic, Aurora runs at 2 ACUs; during sale events, it scales to 64 ACUs within seconds.

This reduces idle compute costs while handling ML demand surges gracefully.

Best Practices for ML Workloads on Serverless v2

- **Use connection pooling**: Use **Amazon RDS Proxy** to manage thousands of short-lived inference queries.

- **Batch feature queries**: Reduce per-connection overhead by grouping multiple predictions into fewer queries.

- **Isolate workloads**: Use custom endpoints or read replicas to separate inference from training feature extraction.

- **Tune scaling limits**: Adjust `MinCapacity` and `MaxCapacity` based on workload patterns (e.g., 2–64 ACUs).

- **Tag model-serving queries** in SQL for observability:

```
SELECT /*ml_inference*/ * FROM
fetch_user_features(...);
```

Performance Considerations

Recommendation	Details
Prefer simple, indexed queries	Keep inference latency low
Use Aurora ML sparingly in loops	Offload batch scoring to SageMaker Pipelines
Monitor with Performance Insights	Identify slow queries, locks, or connection spikes
Warm-up with canary queries	Pre-load caches if traffic is predictable

Cost Optimization

- Pay only for capacity used (measured in ACU-seconds)

- Scale to zero is **not supported** in v2—minimum ACUs apply

- Set `AutoPause=false` for low-latency workloads; set `AutoPause=true` for low-traffic dev/test

- Combine with **Graviton-based db.serverless** for lower ACU costs

Security and Access Control

- Use **IAM roles** for Aurora ML function calls to SageMaker or Comprehend

- Encrypt data with **KMS** (Aurora, S3, SageMaker)

- Apply **VPC security groups** to control inbound/outbound ML endpoint access

Monitoring and Troubleshooting

Use CloudWatch and Performance Insights to:

- Track CPU usage and capacity scaling

- Identify query spikes from ML inference loads

- View connection pressure and latency

- Set alarms for cost or performance anomalies

Limitations and Notes

Limitation	Notes
No scale-to-zero	Minimum ACUs always run
IOPS not configurable	Aurora abstracts storage I/O
Engine versions	Aurora PostgreSQL 13.6+ or MySQL 8.0.23+
Availability	Not yet available in all regions (check Region Support)

Summary

Aurora Serverless v2 is a strong match for **AI/ML applications** that require **burst capacity, cost control, and real-time database interaction**. It simplifies ML infrastructure by scaling database resources only when needed—perfect for unpredictable inference and feature workloads.

Use ASv2 when:

- ML inference spikes are **event-driven or unpredictable**

- You want to **automate scaling** without overprovisioning

- You're building **modern serverless ML apps** or **feature APIs**

Chapter 11: Secure ML Workflows with RDS Proxy and IAM

Machine learning applications increasingly involve real-time interaction with databases—whether for feature retrieval, prediction logging, or feedback collection. These workflows often involve high concurrency and short-lived connections, especially in architectures using AWS Lambda, API Gateway, or SageMaker endpoints. Ensuring **secure, scalable, and efficient** access to Amazon Aurora in such contexts is critical.

This chapter focuses on using **Amazon RDS Proxy** and **IAM database authentication** to secure ML workflows without sacrificing performance. You'll learn how to protect database credentials, manage connections efficiently, and integrate secure access control into ML model serving pipelines and applications.

Why Secure ML Workflows Matter

- **Multiple users/services** may interact with Aurora for feature retrieval or inference.

- **Hardcoding credentials** is a security risk and a management burden.

- **Burst traffic** from Lambda or containerized models can overwhelm Aurora with connections.

- ML pipelines need to **track access, encrypt data, and scale securely**.

Amazon RDS Proxy is a **fully managed connection pooling service** that:

- Sits between your app and Aurora

- Maintains a pool of DB connections

- Supports IAM authentication and Secrets Manager

- Handles failovers and connection reuse seamlessly

It reduces **database connection overhead**, improves **availability**, and enhances **security** by **abstracting direct access** to the database.

Architecture with ML App:

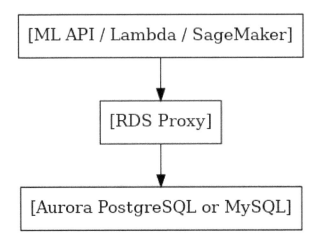

Benefits of RDS Proxy for ML Workflows

- **Connection pooling**: Supports thousands of short-lived queries (e.g., per-inference)

- **Secure access**: Removes need for static DB credentials

- **Failover protection**: Automatically handles Aurora failovers

- **IAM integration**: Enables credential-free authentication with fine-grained roles

---

Typical ML Scenarios Benefiting from RDS Proxy

Scenario   **Benefit**

Lambda-based model serving	Avoids creating a new connection per invocation
Real-time recommendation engine	Reduces latency under burst load
Feedback ingestion from mobile/web apps	Securely handles concurrent writes
SageMaker inference pipelines	Authenticates via IAM, avoids static credentials
Event-driven feature refresh	Supports concurrent queries via one pooled proxy

Step-by-Step: Setting Up RDS Proxy for Aurora ML Apps

1. Create an IAM Role for Proxy Access

```
aws iam create-role \
  --role-name AuroraMLProxyRole \
  --assume-role-policy-document
file://trust-policy.json
```

Example trust policy (Lambda/SageMaker):

```
{
  "Version": "2012-10-17",
  "Statement": [{
    "Effect": "Allow",
```

```
    "Principal": {
       "Service": ["lambda.amazonaws.com",
"sagemaker.amazonaws.com"]
    },
    "Action": "sts:AssumeRole"
  }]
}
```

Attach RDS IAM and Secrets Manager permissions.

---

2. Enable IAM DB Authentication on Aurora

```
aws rds modify-db-cluster \
   --db-cluster-identifier my-ml-cluster \
   --enable-iam-database-authentication \
   --apply-immediately
```

Ensure your Aurora users are created with IDENTIFIED
WITH AWSAuthenticationPlugin.

---

3. Create the RDS Proxy

```
aws rds create-db-proxy \
   --db-proxy-name ml-proxy \
   --engine-family POSTGRESQL \
```

```
  --auth
"AuthScheme=IAM,SecretArn=<secret-
arn>,IAMAuth=REQUIRED" \
  --role-arn
arn:aws:iam::<account>:role/AuroraMLProxyR
ole \
  --vpc-subnet-ids subnet-abc,subnet-def
```

- Attach to Aurora cluster using `aws rds register-db-proxy-targets`

- Add Secrets Manager entry for DB user if needed

---

4. Use Proxy Endpoint in ML Code

Update your application or Lambda to use the **proxy endpoint**, not the raw Aurora endpoint.

Python Example (psycopg2 for Aurora PostgreSQL):

```
import boto3
import psycopg2

token =
boto3.client('rds').generate_db_auth_token
(
    DBHostname='ml-proxy.proxy-xyz.us-
east-1.rds.amazonaws.com',
```

```
    Port=5432,
    DBUsername='ml_user'
)

conn = psycopg2.connect(
    host='ml-proxy.proxy-xyz.us-east-
1.rds.amazonaws.com',
    user='ml_user',
    password=token,
    dbname='ml_db',
    sslmode='require'
)
```

> ⚠ IAM tokens expire after 15 minutes—only use them in short-lived services like Lambda, API Gateway, or batch scoring jobs.

Security Best Practices

- **Use Secrets Manager** for managing non-IAM DB credentials

- Restrict RDS Proxy access via **VPC security groups**

- Enable **TLS/SSL encryption** for proxy-to-client and proxy-to-Aurora traffic

- Use **CloudTrail** to audit authentication and proxy access events

- Rotate IAM roles and secrets on a schedule (e.g., every 90 days)

IAM Role Access Mapping in Aurora

To control DB access via IAM roles:

```
CREATE USER ml_user IDENTIFIED WITH
AWSAuthenticationPlugin AS 'RDS';
GRANT SELECT, EXECUTE ON ALL TABLES IN
SCHEMA public TO ml_user;
```

Map the IAM role to this user in IAM policy:

```
{
  "Version": "2012-10-17",
  "Statement": [{
    "Effect": "Allow",
    "Action": "rds-db:connect",
    "Resource": "arn:aws:rds-db:us-east-
1:123456789012:dbuser:my-db-cluster-
123/ml_user"
  }]
}
```

Observability and Monitoring

- **CloudWatch metrics** for proxy connections, failures, throttles

- **Performance Insights** shows query performance behind the proxy

- Use **RDS Enhanced Monitoring** to track backend usage

- Alert on max connections, failovers, or long query durations

Limitations and Considerations

Limitation	Detail
Max connections per proxy	~5000 concurrent (soft limit)
Write latency	Slight increase (~milliseconds) due to connection pool management
IAM token usage	Not ideal for long-lived services— rotate or use Secrets Manager

| Feature support | Aurora ML functions work seamlessly behind the proxy |

Summary

RDS Proxy combined with IAM authentication is a best-in-class solution for securing and scaling ML workflows that access Amazon Aurora. It simplifies connection management, enforces security boundaries, and reduces overhead—especially for event-driven or containerized ML apps.

Use RDS Proxy + IAM when:

- You're running **high-concurrency, low-latency ML inference**

- You want **secure, passwordless database access**

- Your apps are serverless, containerized, or ephemeral

Part III – NoSQL and Document Databases for AI/ML

Chapter 12: Generative AI and No-Code ML with SageMaker Canvas

Amazon DocumentDB (with MongoDB compatibility) integrates natively with **Amazon SageMaker Canvas**, enabling business analysts, developers, and ML practitioners to harness **no-code ML** and **Generative AI (GenAI)** capabilities on semi-structured data stored in DocumentDB. This chapter explores a practical workflow to use Amazon DocumentDB as a source for ML models in SageMaker Canvas, and outlines how to architect an AI/ML pipeline using these managed services.

Overview

SageMaker Canvas provides a visual interface for building, training, and deploying machine learning models **without writing code**. With native support for Amazon DocumentDB, you can directly use document-oriented data as input for ML pipelines.

In this chapter, we will cover:

- Configuring SageMaker and DocumentDB for integration

- Managing access and roles

106

- Using no-code tools to build predictive models

- Use cases and best practices for GenAI on document data

---

1. Architecture Overview

Here's a high-level architecture for integrating DocumentDB with SageMaker Canvas:

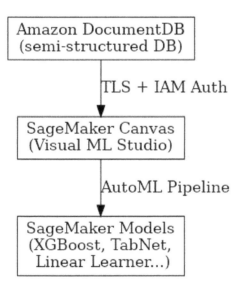

- **Amazon DocumentDB** acts as a source for semi-structured training data.

- **SageMaker Canvas** enables data exploration, labeling, training, and deployment via a UI.

- **SageMaker** back-end trains models using managed infrastructure and scalable ML algorithms.

Setup and Configuration

Prerequisites

- An Amazon DocumentDB cluster with MongoDB 5.0 compatibility.

- A SageMaker Domain and User Profile configured.

- An IAM role with necessary permissions.

Refer to the [Developer Guide] sections:

- **"Configuring the SageMaker AI domain and user profile"**

- **"Configuring IAM access permissions for Amazon DocumentDB and SageMaker AI Canvas".**

IAM Role Permissions

Create a role with the following permissions:

```json
{
  "Version": "2012-10-17",
  "Statement": [
    {
      "Effect": "Allow",
      "Action": [
        "docdb:Connect",
        "docdb:DescribeDBClusters",
        "docdb:DescribeDBInstances",
        "secretsmanager:GetSecretValue",
        "kms:Decrypt"
      ],
      "Resource": "*"
    }
  ]
}
```

Attach this role to the SageMaker user profile.

Ingesting DocumentDB Data into SageMaker Canvas

Creating Database Users

Ensure a **read-only** user is created in Amazon DocumentDB for SageMaker Canvas access:

```
use admin

db.createUser({

  user: "canvasReader",

  pwd: "secure-password",

  roles: [{ role: "readAnyDatabase", db:
"admin" }]

})
```

Configuring Connection in Canvas

1. Open **SageMaker Canvas**

2. Navigate to **Data** > **Connect to new data source**

3. Select **Amazon DocumentDB**

4. Provide:

   o **Cluster endpoint**

- Port (default: 27017)

- Database name

- Authentication method (username/password or Secrets Manager)

- TLS enabled

- Read-only user credentials

Building No-Code ML Models

Once connected, follow these steps in Canvas:

Importing Data

Canvas allows previewing and selecting collections (tables). You can:

- Filter fields

- Clean missing values

- Perform feature engineering (e.g., one-hot encoding, transformations)

Model Building

You can choose:

- **Prediction type**: Binary classification, multiclass, regression

- **Target column**: Label from your data

- **Training settings**: Quick or Standard

Canvas will automatically select and tune algorithms using AutoML under the hood.

Model Evaluation

Canvas generates metrics like:

- ROC AUC

- Confusion Matrix

- Precision/Recall

- RMSE (for regression)

Models can be shared or exported to SageMaker Studio for code-based refinement.

Use Cases for Generative AI on DocumentDB

With recent support for **vector search** in DocumentDB 5.0, you can extend AI workflows to GenAI applications:

Example: Product Search with Vector Embeddings

- Store **product descriptions** as text documents in DocumentDB

- Generate **embeddings** using an Amazon SageMaker model

- Use $vectorSearch to power semantic search interfaces

```
{
  "$vectorSearch": {
    "queryVector": [0.12, 0.54, ...],
    "index": "product_vectors",
    "limit": 5,
    "numCandidates": 100
  }
}
```

Reference: **Vector Search** section in the DocumentDB Developer Guide.

Best Practices

Data Modeling

- Flatten documents for better compatibility with tabular ML models

- Use JSON schema validation to enforce structure

Access Control

- Use IAM authentication with short-lived tokens

- Store credentials in **AWS Secrets Manager**

Scaling

- Use **read replicas** to serve ML data without impacting transactional load

- Monitor performance using **CloudWatch metrics** like `ReadIOPS`, `CPUUtilization`

Cost Optimization

- Enable **I/O-optimized** storage for ML-heavy workloads

- Clean up temporary collections used for feature generation

Real-World Scenario

Customer Support AI Assistant

- Ingest customer tickets from a web portal into DocumentDB

- Use SageMaker Canvas to build a classifier for:

  - Priority prediction (low/medium/high)

  - Routing (department tags)

- Use vector search for FAQ matching in real time

- Integrate with a chatbot (e.g., Amazon Lex)

Conclusion

By integrating Amazon DocumentDB with SageMaker Canvas, organizations can operationalize AI/ML on rich JSON data without writing code. Whether it's building predictive models or powering GenAI experiences with vector search, this combination accelerates time-to-insight while preserving governance and scalability.

Chapter 13: Implementing Vector Search in DocumentDB

As AI applications increasingly require semantic understanding and similarity search, **vector search** has become a critical capability in modern databases. With the release of **Amazon DocumentDB 5.0**, AWS introduced native support for **vector search**, allowing developers to efficiently perform **approximate nearest neighbor (ANN)** queries on high-dimensional embeddings stored alongside JSON document data.

In this chapter, we will walk through the architecture, configuration, and best practices for implementing vector search in Amazon DocumentDB, particularly in the context of AI/ML workflows.

Introduction to Vector Search

Vector search allows you to find items in a dataset that are most similar to a given vector, which typically represents text, image, audio, or other high-dimensional data encoded using an ML model (e.g., sentence transformers or image encoders).

Use Cases

- **Semantic product search**: Retrieve similar items based on description.

- **Conversational AI**: Match user input to knowledge base answers.

- **Personalization and recommendation**: Find similar users or products.

- **Image similarity**: Match a query image with similar stored images.

How Vector Search Works in DocumentDB

Amazon DocumentDB uses an **approximate nearest neighbor (ANN)** algorithm for indexing and querying vectors. The feature is accessed using a special **aggregation operator:** $vectorSearch.

Key Components

- **Vector field**: A field in the document that stores an array of floats (the embedding).

- **Vector index**: An index created on the vector field to enable fast similarity queries.

- **$vectorSearch**: An aggregation stage that returns the most similar vectors to a query vector.

Architecture Overview

Here's how a vector search pipeline typically works:

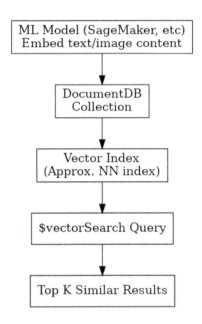

Creating and Populating a Vector-Enabled Collection

Example Document

```
{
  "_id": "doc1",
  "title": "Building a chatbot with AWS",
  "embedding": [0.13, -0.22, 0.55, ...]
// Float vector of fixed length
}
```

Inserting Vectors via Python

```python
from pymongo import MongoClient
import boto3

client = MongoClient('mongodb://<username>:<password>@<cluster-endpoint>:27017/?tls=true')
db = client['ml_docs']
collection = db['knowledge_base']

doc = {
    "_id": "doc1",
    "title": "Chatbot development with AWS",
    "embedding": [0.15, -0.42, 0.63, ...]  # Typically 128 to 1536 dimensions
}
collection.insert_one(doc)
```

Creating a Vector Index

You must explicitly create a **vector index** on the target field. Use the `createIndex` command:

```
db.knowledge_base.createIndex(
  { embedding: "vector" },
  {
    name: "embedding_index",
    defaultSimilarityMetric: "cosine",
    dimensions: 1536,  // Match embedding size from model
    numPartitions: 1,
    numProbes: 1
  }
)
```

> ⚠ The number of dimensions must match the length of the embedding arrays stored.

Index Parameters:

- `dimensions`: Vector length

- `defaultSimilarityMetric`: "cosine" | "euclidean" | "dotProduct"

- `numPartitions`: Affects indexing granularity and performance

- numProbes: Determines query thoroughness (trade-off between speed and accuracy)

Performing a Vector Search Query

Use the $vectorSearch stage within an aggregation pipeline:

```
db.knowledge_base.aggregate([
  {
    $vectorSearch: {
      queryVector: [0.13, -0.22, 0.55,
...],
      path: "embedding",
      k: 5,
      index: "embedding_index",
      numCandidates: 100
    }
  },
  { $project: { _id: 1, title: 1, score: {
$meta: "vectorSearchScore" } } }
])
```

- `k`: Number of nearest neighbors to return

- `numCandidates`: Number of candidate vectors to scan

- `$meta: "vectorSearchScore"` returns the similarity score

Best Practices for Vector Search

Choosing the Right Embeddings

- Use **SageMaker JumpStart** or **pretrained HuggingFace models** to encode your content.

- Normalize vectors for cosine similarity (if not done by the model).

Index Tuning

- Start with `numPartitions=1` and `numProbes=1`, then tune based on accuracy/performance needs.

- Avoid excessive dimensionality (>1536) unless required.

Data Modeling

- Embed vectors as a separate field (`embedding`)

- Store metadata alongside for filtering or display

```
{
  "_id": "faq123",
  "question": "How do I reset my
password?",
  "answer": "Use the password reset link
on the login page.",
  "embedding": [0.11, 0.39, -0.56, ...],
  "tags": ["auth", "password"]
}
```

Integration with AI/ML Workflows

Embedding Generation Pipeline

Use **AWS Lambda** or a **SageMaker processing job** to transform text and store embeddings:

```
from sentence_transformers import
SentenceTransformer

model = SentenceTransformer("all-MiniLM-
L6-v2")

vector = model.encode("Reset my password")
```

```
collection.insert_one({ "question": "Reset
password", "embedding": vector.tolist() })
```

Real-Time Search

Trigger vector search from:

- A chatbot built with **Amazon Lex**

- An API hosted on **Amazon API Gateway + Lambda**

- A Streamlit or React frontend for internal tools

Monitoring and Limitations

Monitoring

Use **CloudWatch metrics** to monitor:

- QueryCount, ReadIOPS, QueryExecutionTime

- Log slow queries using the profiler

Known Limitations

124

- No support for **compound indexes** involving vector fields.

- Maximum vector dimensions: **2048**

- Max vector document size: ~16MB (standard BSON limit)

- Cannot combine $vectorSearch with $lookup directly.

Real-World Example: AI-Powered FAQ Bot

Objective: Implement a bot that answers user queries using semantic search.

Workflow:

1. Store historical FAQ pairs in DocumentDB

2. Generate embeddings using a BERT model (via SageMaker)

3. Index the vector field with createIndex(...)

4. On query, encode user input and run $vectorSearch

5. Return the best match with the highest vector similarity

Summary

Vector search in Amazon DocumentDB brings powerful semantic search capabilities directly into your document database, enabling intelligent, real-time ML-driven applications without needing external vector databases.

By integrating embedding models with DocumentDB collections and utilizing its $vectorSearch operator, developers can streamline AI features such as recommendations, chatbots, and search engines—all within their existing AWS stack.

Chapter 14: Real-Time ML Pipelines with Change Streams and Lambda

In AI/ML architectures, real-time data processing enables immediate insights and responses. For document-centric applications using **Amazon DocumentDB**, integrating **change streams** with **AWS Lambda** offers a scalable and event-driven foundation for **real-time ML pipelines**. This chapter guides you through building such pipelines to trigger model inference, enrichment, or downstream actions in response to document changes.

Overview: Change Streams + Lambda for Real-Time ML

Change streams in Amazon DocumentDB enable applications to **listen to inserts, updates, and deletes** on collections. Combined with **AWS Lambda**, these events can automatically trigger:

- Real-time **model inference** (e.g., sentiment analysis, classification)

- **Data enrichment** (e.g., add embedding vectors or tags)

- **Integration** with other AWS services (e.g., Amazon S3, EventBridge, SNS)

Architecture Diagram

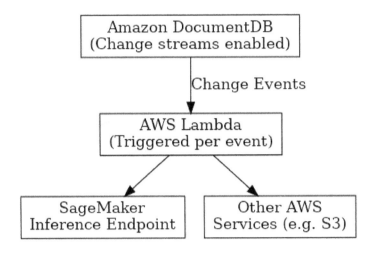

Enabling Change Streams in DocumentDB

Before consuming change events, you must **enable change streams** on the target collection:

Modify the Cluster Parameter Group

```
aws docdb modify-db-cluster-parameter-
group \
  --db-cluster-parameter-group-name my-
docdb-pg \
```

128

```
  --parameters
"ParameterName=change_stream_log_retention
_duration,ParameterValue=432000,ApplyMetho
d=immediate"
```

- change_stream_log_retention_duration:
  Specifies the retention in seconds (max: 604800 =
  7 days)

Create a Change Stream Collection

Change streams can be consumed via the MongoDB-compatible driver:

```
pipeline = [{'$match': {'operationType':
{'$in': ['insert', 'update']}}}]

with collection.watch(pipeline) as stream:

    for change in stream:

        print(change)
```

Integrating Change Streams with AWS Lambda

Amazon DocumentDB does not natively emit events to Lambda. You must **deploy a listener application**, typically on **Amazon EC2**, **AWS Fargate**, or a container on **EKS**, that:

1. Connects to the change stream

2. Forwards events to a Lambda function or Step Functions

Example Listener in Python

```python
from pymongo import MongoClient
import boto3
import json

client =
MongoClient("mongodb://<user>:<password>@<
endpoint>:27017/?tls=true")
collection = client.mydb.mycollection
lambda_client = boto3.client("lambda")

for change in collection.watch():
    lambda_client.invoke(
        FunctionName="docdb-change-
processor",
        InvocationType="Event",

Payload=json.dumps(change).encode("utf-8")
    )
```

Use long polling and exponential backoff in production.

AWS Lambda: Real-Time Inference Example

You can build a Lambda function to process change events and trigger ML inference, such as text classification.

Sample Lambda Handler

```python
import json
import boto3

runtime = boto3.client("sagemaker-runtime")

def lambda_handler(event, context):
    for record in event['Records']:
        change = json.loads(record['body'])
        text = change['fullDocument']['message']

        response = runtime.invoke_endpoint(
```

```
            EndpointName='my-text-
classifier',

ContentType='application/json',
            Body=json.dumps({'text':
text})
        )


    prediction =
json.loads(response['Body'].read())
        print("Prediction:", prediction)


        # Optionally update DocumentDB
```

Permissions

Ensure the Lambda has permissions to:

- Invoke SageMaker
  (sagemaker:InvokeEndpoint)

- Access DocumentDB (if updating documents)

- Log to CloudWatch

Event Filtering and Routing

You can apply **filters** in your change stream or routing logic:

- Filter by operationType (insert, update, delete)

- Filter by ns.coll (collection name)

- Route based on field values (e.g., only infer on "status=unprocessed")

Example Filter Pipeline

```
pipeline = [{
    "$match": {
        "operationType": "insert",
        "fullDocument.status": "new"
    }
}]
```

Persisting Inference Results Back to DocumentDB

You can enrich documents with ML metadata directly from Lambda:

```
collection.update_one(
    {"_id": doc_id},
```

```
    {"$set": {"classification": result,
"processedAt": datetime.utcnow()}}
)
```

Use **optimistic concurrency** (e.g., $setOnInsert) or
timestamps to prevent conflicts.

Scaling and Resilience

Listener Process

- Deploy as a **long-running container** (ECS, EKS)

- Use **process supervision** (e.g., supervisord, systemd)

- Handle **reconnection** and **resume tokens** to avoid data loss

Lambda

- Avoid long-running inferences; use **async endpoints** if needed

- Batch events if using **Amazon SQS or EventBridge** as an intermediate layer

Monitoring and Observability

DocumentDB Metrics (via CloudWatch)

- `ChangeStreamsActive`

- `ChangeStreamsErrors`

- `LowMemThrottleQueueDepth`

Lambda Logs (via CloudWatch Logs)

- Monitor execution time and errors

Recommended Alerts

- Lambda errors or timeouts

- EC2 listener failures

- High replica lag on DocumentDB

Real-World Use Case: Real-Time Moderation

Scenario: A social media app stores user posts in DocumentDB. Each new post triggers a sentiment classifier.

Flow

1. User posts a message → inserted into DocumentDB

2. Change stream detects insert

3. Lambda invokes a sentiment analysis model (SageMaker)

4. Classification (positive/negative) stored back in DocumentDB

5. Posts marked "negative" are queued for moderation

This enables **automated moderation queues** with no polling or batch delays.

Summary

By combining **DocumentDB change streams** with **AWS Lambda**, you can build responsive and intelligent ML pipelines that trigger based on real-time data events. This pattern is ideal for:

- Continuous inference

- Dynamic enrichment

- Event-driven architecture

It minimizes latency and infrastructure complexity by using serverless patterns and managed services.

Chapter 15: Validating ML Input Data with JSON Schema

In machine learning systems, **data quality** is a foundational requirement. Poor or inconsistent data inputs can degrade model performance, introduce bias, and complicate feature engineering. When using **Amazon DocumentDB** to store ML inputs, leveraging **JSON Schema validation** ensures the structural and semantic correctness of your data **before ingestion** into training pipelines or real-time inference systems.

This chapter explores how to use DocumentDB's JSON Schema validation to enforce structure on semi-structured data—especially in ML-driven applications where inputs must conform to specific schemas for feature extraction, embedding generation, and model inference.

Why Validate ML Input Data?

Validating input documents helps ML pipelines by:

- Preventing missing or malformed fields that break preprocessing or training

- Ensuring correct **types** (e.g., numeric, categorical)

- Enforcing consistent structure for embedding or vectorization

- Avoiding garbage-in, garbage-out (GIGO) scenarios in model development

138

By enforcing **field-level constraints** at the database layer, DocumentDB reduces data preparation effort and increases trust in ML pipelines.

Overview of JSON Schema Validation in DocumentDB

Amazon DocumentDB supports **MongoDB-compatible JSON Schema validation**, enabling developers to specify:

- Required fields

- Data types (string, number, array, etc.)

- Value formats and constraints (e.g., ranges, patterns)

- Nested document structure

Validation is enforced on `insert` and `update` operations when configured.

Creating a Schema Validator

To apply a validation schema to a collection, use the following command when creating it:

Example: User Feedback Data for Sentiment Model

```
{
  "$jsonSchema": {
    "bsonType": "object",
    "required": ["userId", "message",
"timestamp"],
    "properties": {
      "userId": {
        "bsonType": "string",
        "description": "must be a string
and is required"
      },
      "message": {
        "bsonType": "string",
        "minLength": 3,
        "description": "free-form text for
sentiment analysis"
      },
      "timestamp": {
        "bsonType": "date",
        "description": "submission time"
      },
      "metadata": {
```

```
      "bsonType": "object",
      "properties": {
        "device": { "bsonType": "string"
},
        "geo": { "bsonType": "objectId"
}
      }
    }
  }
 }
}
```

```
db.createCollection("feedback", {
  validator: {
    $jsonSchema: { /* insert schema JSON
above */ }
  }
})
```

Once applied, invalid documents will be **rejected with an error**.

Enforcing Validation on Existing Collections

To apply validation to a collection you've already created:

```
db.runCommand({
  collMod: "feedback",
  validator: {
    $jsonSchema: { /* schema JSON */ }
  },
  validationLevel: "strict", // or
"moderate"
  validationAction: "error"  // or "warn"
})
```

- `validationLevel: "strict"` — validates inserts and updates (default)

- `validationAction: "error"` — rejects invalid documents (default)

Use `"warn"` for soft enforcement during migration periods.

Schema for ML Input Documents

Example: Product Vector Document

```json
{
  "$jsonSchema": {
    "bsonType": "object",
    "required": ["productId", "description",
"embedding"],
    "properties": {
      "productId": {
        "bsonType": "string"
      },
      "description": {
        "bsonType": "string"
      },
      "embedding": {
        "bsonType": "array",
        "items": {
          "bsonType": "double"
        },
        "minItems": 128,
        "maxItems": 1536
      }
```

143

```
    }
  }
}
```

This schema ensures that:

- The product has a valid string ID and description

- Embedding is a floating-point array within a dimensionality range suitable for vector search

---

Validating Documents from External Sources

If your pipeline ingests user-submitted, external, or third-party data (e.g., via API Gateway or S3 ETL), schema validation in DocumentDB acts as a **first line of defense** before corruption spreads downstream.

Real-Time Use Case

1. API posts new user data to Lambda

2. Lambda inserts document into DocumentDB

3. If invalid, insert fails and logs issue

4. Valid data automatically flows to ML pipeline

Validation and Change Streams

Validated collections can still emit **change stream events**. If a document insert or update fails due to schema violations, **no change event is emitted**, keeping your stream consumers clean.

This is especially useful in **real-time inference pipelines** (see Chapter 14), where only valid events should trigger downstream actions.

8. Best Practices

☑ Start with "warn" Mode for Iterative Adoption

```
validationAction: "warn"
```

Use this during schema rollout to identify violations without blocking operations.

☑ Use Schema Validation for Training Data Integrity

Ensure your training datasets stored in DocumentDB conform to strict schema rules. This prevents:

145

- Feature mismatch

- Label leakage

- Type errors in vector generation

Combine with Indexes for Efficient Querying

Schema-validated fields are **indexable**. You can safely index fields like `embedding`, `timestamp`, or `category` without worrying about mixed types.

```
db.feedback.createIndex({ timestamp: 1 })
```

☑ Use Nested Schema for Complex Documents

```
"features": {
  "bsonType": "object",
  "properties": {
    "clicks": { "bsonType": "int" },
    "views": { "bsonType": "int" }
  }
}
```

This ensures nested fields are well-formed before being vectorized or joined downstream.

Avoid Overconstraining Optional ML Metadata

If fields like `"score"` or `"label"` are added later by inference functions, make them optional in the schema. You can still validate their types without requiring presence:

```
"score": {
  "bsonType": ["double", "null"]
}
```

Limitations

- No support for advanced conditional logic (`if-then-else` rules)

- Cannot enforce string patterns or enum values

- Cannot validate cross-field relationships (e.g., `score` must exist if `label` exists)

See full limitations in the **Amazon DocumentDB Developer Guide – JSON Schema Validation section**.

Summary

By enforcing JSON Schema validation in Amazon DocumentDB, ML teams can:

- Safeguard input quality

- Reduce preprocessing and cleanup overhead

- Catch bad data early

- Improve consistency across training and inference pipelines

This approach empowers teams to treat **semi-structured documents with the same rigor** as structured tabular data—critical in production-grade ML systems.

Chapter 16: Aggregation Pipelines for Data Transformation

In ML and AI systems, preparing data often involves complex transformations: filtering, reshaping, grouping, or feature extraction. These tasks can be efficiently performed directly within **Amazon DocumentDB** using **aggregation pipelines**, eliminating the need to export data to separate processing engines.

Amazon DocumentDB supports the **MongoDB aggregation framework**, allowing powerful and expressive data processing operations over documents—ideal for transforming raw JSON data into ML-ready features, summaries, or statistics.

This chapter explores how to design and optimize **aggregation pipelines** for machine learning workflows in Amazon DocumentDB.

What Are Aggregation Pipelines?

An **aggregation pipeline** is a sequence of stages, each transforming the document stream. Think of it as a **functional data transformation chain**—similar to Unix pipes or SQL window functions.

Each stage takes input documents, processes them, and passes output to the next stage.

- Feature engineering (bucketing, encoding, normalization)

- Labeling or annotation pipelines

- Time-series transformations (e.g., rolling windows)

- Class or event frequency calculation

- Pre-aggregation for training datasets

Basic Pipeline Structure

Syntax

```
db.collection.aggregate([
  { $match: { ... } },
  { $project: { ... } },
  { $group: { _id: ..., aggField: { $sum:
... } } },

  ...
])
```

Each stage is a document with a single operator (e.g., $match, $project, $group).

Example: Building a Training Dataset

Let's say your collection stores user interactions:

```
{
  "_id": "abc123",
  "userId": "u42",
  "itemId": "i99",
  "event": "click",
  "timestamp": ISODate("2025-03-
01T12:34:00Z")
}
```

Goal: Count user events per item as training features.

```
db.interactions.aggregate([
  { $match: { timestamp: { $gte:
ISODate("2025-01-01") } } },
  { $group: {
      _id: { user: "$userId", item:
"$itemId" },
      click_count: { $sum: { $cond: [ {
$eq: ["$event", "click"] }, 1, 0 ] } },
      view_count: { $sum: { $cond: [ {
$eq: ["$event", "view"] }, 1, 0 ] } }
  }},
  { $project: {
```

```
      user: "$_id.user",
      item: "$_id.item",
      click_count: 1,
      view_count: 1,
      _id: 0
  }}
])
```

This outputs documents like:

```
{
  "user": "u42",
  "item": "i99",
  "click_count": 5,
  "view_count": 12
}
```

Perfect for feature ingestion into an ML model.

Supported Operators in Amazon DocumentDB

DocumentDB supports a rich set of aggregation operators, including:

Stage Operators

- `$match` – filter documents

- `$project` – shape fields

- `$group` – aggregate

- `$sort`, `$limit`, `$skip`

- `$unwind` – flatten arrays

- `$addFields` – derive new fields

- `$setWindowFields` – sliding window analytics (5.0+)

Expression Operators

- Arithmetic: `$add`, `$multiply`, `$subtract`

- Conditional: `$cond`, `$ifNull`, `$switch`

- String: `$concat`, `$substr`, `$toLower`

- Date: `$year`, `$month`, `$dateDiff`

- Array: `$size`, `$filter`, `$map`

- Accumulators: `$sum`, `$avg`, `$max`, `$stdDevPop`

Reference: [Aggregation Pipeline Operators section in Developer Guide]

Example: Feature Binning and Encoding

Normalize timestamps to hour-of-day buckets

```
db.events.aggregate([
  { $project: {
      userId: 1,
      hour: { $hour: "$timestamp" }
  }},
  { $group: {
      _id: "$hour",
      event_count: { $sum: 1 }
  }},
  { $sort: { _id: 1 } }
])
```

This could help in building **time-of-day activity features** for a model.

Using $lookup for Feature Joins

Amazon DocumentDB 5.0+ supports $lookup for joining across collections.

Join User Profile to Interaction Logs

154

```
db.interactions.aggregate([
  { $match: { event: "click" } },
  { $lookup: {
      from: "users",
      localField: "userId",
      foreignField: "_id",
      as: "user_info"
  }},
  { $unwind: "$user_info" },
  { $project: {
      userId: 1,
      itemId: 1,
      age: "$user_info.age",
      gender: "$user_info.gender"
  }}
])
```

Use this to **enrich event logs** with demographic features prior to ML processing.

Advanced: Window Functions for Time-Series ML

Amazon DocumentDB 5.0 introduces $setWindowFields.

Rolling Event Count Over Time

```
db.interactions.aggregate([
  { $setWindowFields: {
      partitionBy: "$userId",
      sortBy: { timestamp: 1 },
      output: {
        click_rolling_sum: {
          $sum: {
            $cond: [{ $eq: ["$event",
"click"] }, 1, 0]
          },
          window: { documents: [-5, 0] }
        }
      }
  }}
])
```

Useful for modeling **recency**, **frequency**, or **session-based behaviors** in ML tasks.

Feature Transformation Pipeline Example

Let's walk through a **complete transformation** to build a training dataset:

1. **Filter** recent events

2. **Join** user metadata

3. **Group** events by user/item

4. **Compute** frequency features

5. **Export** for ML

```
db.interactions.aggregate([
  { $match: { timestamp: { $gte:
ISODate("2025-01-01") } } },
  { $lookup: {
      from: "users",
      localField: "userId",
      foreignField: "_id",
      as: "user"
  }},
  { $unwind: "$user" },
  { $group: {
      _id: { userId: "$userId", itemId:
"$itemId" },
      clicks: { $sum: { $cond: [ { $eq:
["$event", "click"] }, 1, 0 ] } },
      views: { $sum: { $cond: [ { $eq:
["$event", "view"] }, 1, 0 ] } },
```

```
            age: { $first: "$user.age" },
            gender: { $first: "$user.gender" }
    }},
    { $project: {
            user: "$_id.userId",
            item: "$_id.itemId",
            clicks: 1,
            views: 1,
            age: 1,
            gender: 1,
            _id: 0
    }}
])
```

Best Practices

- **Project early**: Use $project to remove unneeded fields early in the pipeline.

- **Use indexes**: Ensure $match filters use indexed fields.

- **Avoid deep nesting**: Flatten documents before heavy grouping.

- **Paginate large pipelines**: Use $limit and $skip for batch processing.

- **Combine with $out** to persist results:

```
{ $out: "training_features" }
```

Real-World Use Case: Training Data Generation

Scenario: An e-commerce system logs user behavior in a clickstream collection.

Solution: Use aggregation to extract session summaries, encode time, join user segments, and create a training_dataset collection consumed by SageMaker.

Benefits:

- No ETL needed

- DocumentDB handles filtering and feature engineering

- Consistent, versioned pipelines

Summary

Amazon DocumentDB's aggregation pipelines provide a powerful, in-database transformation engine ideal for ML tasks like feature extraction, user segmentation, and time-based analytics.

They reduce operational complexity by allowing **data engineering to happen directly where the data lives**, and align perfectly with AI/ML workflows that demand fresh, structured, and feature-rich datasets.

Chapter 17: NLP & Geo Models with Text and Geospatial Search

Machine learning applications often need to blend **natural language processing (NLP)** with **location awareness**—for example, recommending local services based on a query, or classifying support tickets by both content and origin. Amazon DocumentDB natively supports **text search** and **geospatial querying**, enabling developers to build powerful NLP and location-based ML models without requiring separate search engines or GIS systems.

In this chapter, we explore how to store, query, and transform unstructured text and spatial data in Amazon DocumentDB, and how to integrate these features into AI/ML workflows for tasks like semantic search, regional recommendations, and NLP model training.

Overview: Search Meets Location

By combining text and location features in your data model, you can:

- Power **local search experiences** ("pizza near me" queries)

- Preprocess **training data** for NLP classification models (e.g., location-specific sentiment)

- Filter or enrich **vector embeddings** based on user region or geofencing

- Use text content and geolocation as **joint inputs** to multi-modal models

Amazon DocumentDB supports:

Capability	Operator	Notes
Full-text search	`$text`	Requires text index
Geospatial point-in-radius	`$geoWithin`, `$nearSphere`	Works with `2dsphere` index
Combined filtering	`$and`, `$match`	Compose text and geo filters

Modeling Text and Location Data

Here's a sample document structure for a business listing:

```
{
  "_id": "biz42",
  "name": "Sunrise Bakery",
  "description": "Fresh sourdough and
croissants every morning.",
  "tags": ["bakery", "breakfast", "coffee"],
  "location": {
    "type": "Point",
    "coordinates": [-122.4194, 37.7749] //
[longitude, latitude]
```

```
    }
}
```

This structure supports:

- Text search on `description, tags`

- Geospatial search on `location`

To use full-text search, create a **text index**:

```
db.businesses.createIndex({ description:
"text", tags: "text" })
```

```
db.businesses.find({
  $text: { $search: "sourdough croissant"
}
})
```

You can return a text match **score** using projection:

163

```
db.businesses.find(
  { $text: { $search: "croissant" } },
  { score: { $meta: "textScore" }, name: 1
}
).sort({ score: { $meta: "textScore" } })
```

Enabling Geospatial Search

Create a **2dsphere** index on the `location` field:

```
db.businesses.createIndex({ location:
"2dsphere" })
```

Query Example: Nearby Results

```
db.businesses.find({
  location: {
    $nearSphere: {
      $geometry: {
        type: "Point",
        coordinates: [-122.42, 37.77]
      },
      $maxDistance: 1000  // in meters
    }
```

```
    }
})
```

Returns businesses within a **1 km radius** of the point.

Combining Text and Location Filters

Amazon DocumentDB allows combining full-text and geo filters:

```
db.businesses.find({
  $text: { $search: "croissant" },
  location: {
    $nearSphere: {
      $geometry: { type: "Point",
coordinates: [-122.42, 37.77] },
      $maxDistance: 1500
    }
  }
})
```

This is ideal for "search nearby" experiences in mobile or mapping apps.

Feature Engineering for ML

Text and location fields can be transformed into model features:

Text Feature Extraction

- Use Sentence Transformers (e.g., `all-MiniLM`) in SageMaker to embed `description`

- Tokenize tags and build term-frequency vectors

- Count keyword hits per category (e.g., "coffee", "gluten-free")

Location Feature Engineering

- Convert coordinates to **city**, **region**, or **timezone** via reverse geocoding

- Use **clustering** (e.g., DBSCAN) to assign location-based segments

- Bucket into grids or zones (lat/lon rounding)

These features can be used in downstream ML models for:

- Classification (e.g., business type)

- Recommendation (e.g., local preferences)

- Clustering and segmentation

Real-World Example: Geo-Aware Review Classification

Problem: Classify reviews by sentiment, with awareness of the city they're written in.

Pipeline:

1. Store reviews in DocumentDB with:

    - `text`: user review

    - `location`: lat/lon from user device

2. Use `$text` search to pre-label training samples:

    - `"great"` = positive, `"terrible"` = negative

3. Extract:

    - Embedding of `text` (via SageMaker)

    - Location region (e.g., San Francisco)

167

4. Train model:

    - ○ `inputs = [embedding, city_one_hot]`

    - ○ `target = sentiment_label`

5. Deploy with SageMaker Endpoint

Best Practices

Indexing

- Combine `text` and `2dsphere` indexes where applicable.

- Use compound indexes only on non-geo, non-text fields.

Performance Tuning

- Use `$limit` with `$geoWithin` to reduce scan time

- Avoid `$text` + `$regex` together (not supported)

Query Strategy

- Use $text first, then apply $geoWithin in aggregation pipelines for large datasets

- Paginate with skip/limit or timestamp filters

Integrating with ML Pipelines

You can use text and location data from DocumentDB in both batch and real-time pipelines:

Task	Approach
Text Embedding	Use SageMaker NLP models (e.g., BERT)
Geo Enrichment	Use Amazon Location Service or GeoNames
Model Input	Combine embedding + region ID
Serving	Use DocumentDB + Lambda + SageMaker Inference

Summary

Amazon DocumentDB provides native support for both **text search** and **geospatial queries**, making it a versatile data store for AI/ML systems that operate on natural language and location data. By combining these capabilities, you can build intelligent applications that understand **what users want** and **where they are**, all without leaving the DocumentDB ecosystem.

Part IV – Graph Databases for AI/ML

Chapter 18: Introduction to Graph AI/ML Workflows

As AI and machine learning evolve beyond traditional data structures, graph-based data models are becoming essential for uncovering complex relationships, patterns, and structures. In AWS, Neptune Analytics bridges the gap between graph theory and modern data science, offering native support for graph processing at memory scale, integration with vector search, and optimized algorithms for ML-powered insights.

This chapter introduces the foundations of graph-based AI/ML workflows using Amazon Neptune Analytics, providing a blueprint for architecting intelligent, relationship-aware applications in the cloud.

Why Graphs in AI/ML?

Graphs model entities (nodes) and their relationships (edges), enabling representation of real-world systems such as social networks, supply chains, cybersecurity domains, and recommendation systems. Graph-based ML workflows leverage this structure to:

- Discover communities or clusters (e.g., fraud rings, social groups).

- Predict links (e.g., friend suggestions, likely purchases).

171

- Rank nodes by importance (e.g., influence scoring, threat detection).

- Embed graph topologies into vector space for neural processing.

Traditional ML workflows flatten these structures, often losing the nuance of connection-rich data. Graph-based approaches retain that richness, and Neptune Analytics offers the scale and performance to operationalize these workflows.

Neptune Analytics: A Purpose-Built Graph Engine for AI/ML

Amazon Neptune Analytics is optimized for **in-memory graph processing**, providing:

- **Low-latency openCypher query support**.

- **Prebuilt graph algorithms** like PageRank, label propagation, and Jaccard similarity.

- **Vector indexing and search** for embedding-based inference.

- **Massive-scale batch imports** from Amazon S3 or Neptune Database.

- **Managed graph-as-a-service** provisioning with auto-scaling compute.

These features allow ML engineers and data scientists to iterate faster, apply graph theory at scale, and seamlessly integrate Neptune into AI pipelines.

Architecture Overview: A Graph AI Workflow on AWS

A typical graph-based AI/ML architecture using Neptune Analytics includes the following components:

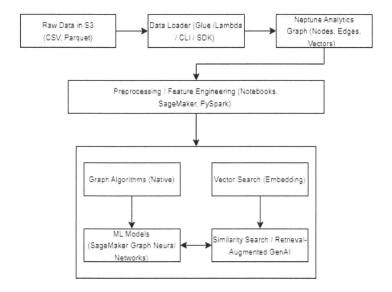

This architecture enables:

- Graph ingestion and enrichment.

- Exploratory data analysis via native queries.

- Feature extraction via graph algorithms.

- Vector search for embedding-based AI (e.g., GenAI applications).

- Seamless export to downstream ML systems like Amazon SageMaker.

Graph-Centric Machine Learning Techniques

Let's walk through key ML techniques empowered by Neptune Analytics:

---

1. Node Classification

Use case: Predict the category or role of a node in a network.

Approach:

- Run algorithms like `.labelPropagation()` to infer communities.

- Use the results as features in downstream classifiers (e.g., SageMaker XGBoost).

```
CALL algo.labelPropagation()
YIELD nodeId, communityId
RETURN nodeId, communityId
```

Export results using AWS CLI for downstream modeling:

```
aws neptune-graph start-export-task \
  --graph-identifier g-abc123 \
  --format CSV \
  --output-location s3://my-bucket/graph-export/
```

---

2. Link Prediction

Use case: Suggest new connections (e.g., friends, transactions).

Approach:

- Use `.jaccardSimilarity()` or `.overlapSimilarity()` to compute edge likelihoods.

```
CALL algo.jaccardSimilarity()
YIELD node1, node2, score
RETURN node1, node2, score
ORDER BY score DESC
LIMIT 10
```

This can drive recommendation engines or fraud detection alerts.

---

3. Centrality and Influence Scoring

Use case: Identify key influencers or critical nodes in a graph.

Approach:

- Algorithms like `.pageRank()` and `.closenessCentrality()` score nodes.

```
CALL algo.pageRank()
YIELD nodeId, score
RETURN nodeId, score
ORDER BY score DESC
```

These scores become features for downstream predictive models.

---

4. Community Detection

Use case: Group users/customers based on structural similarity.

Approach:

- Use `.wcc()` (Weakly Connected Components) or `.labelPropagation()`.

```
CALL algo.wcc()
YIELD componentId, nodeId
RETURN componentId, COUNT(*) as size
ORDER BY size DESC
```

Helps segment user bases for targeted marketing or threat isolation.

---

5. Embedding-Based Vector Search

Use case: Power recommendation engines and GenAI with vector-aware queries.

Approach:

- Load node embeddings into Neptune.

- Use `.vectors.topKByEmbedding()` for similarity search.

177

```
CALL algo.vectors.topKByEmbedding({
  embedding: [0.11, 0.32, 0.44, ...,
0.07],
  k: 5
})
YIELD nodeId, score
RETURN nodeId, score
```

This is especially powerful when integrating with LLMs for retrieval-augmented generation (RAG).

Best Practices for AI/ML with Neptune Analytics

- **Vector indexing**: Preconfigure your graph for vector support (e.g., `--vector-search '{"dimension": 768}'`).

- **Batch preprocessing**: Use AWS Glue or Spark for large-scale preprocessing before ingesting.

- **Graph partitioning**: Keep related entities tightly connected to improve performance.

- **Parameter tuning**: Adjust concurrency, depth, or thresholds for algorithms like PageRank or WCC.

- **Integration**: Export results to S3 for training in SageMaker or consumption by downstream apps.

Real-World Example: Cybersecurity Threat Graph

In a threat detection workflow:

- Nodes represent IPs, hosts, users, malware signatures.

- Edges represent communications, file writes, authentication attempts.

- Algorithms highlight central (potentially malicious) nodes.

- Label propagation finds groups of compromised hosts.

- Vector embeddings let GenAI systems describe threat paths with context.

This rich graph intelligence enables both automated scoring and human-in-the-loop analysis via notebooks.

Integrating Neptune with SageMaker Pipelines

Use Amazon SageMaker for:

- Training ML models using Neptune-exported graph features.

- Running automated pipelines for classification, regression, or clustering.

- Integrating inference back into Neptune to update predictions on the graph.

Example:

```
import boto3
import pandas as pd

s3 = boto3.client("s3")
s3.download_file("my-bucket", "graph-output/features.csv", "features.csv")
df = pd.read_csv("features.csv")

# Train with SageMaker SDK...
```

Summary

Neptune Analytics is a formidable engine for powering intelligent graph-based AI workflows. With its deep integration into the AWS ecosystem and support for both traditional and neural graph techniques, it enables scalable, in-memory reasoning across billions of relationships.

In this chapter, we've established the role of graphs in AI/ML, explored Neptune's core features, and laid out real-world workflows for link prediction, influence scoring, community detection, and embedding-based search. Subsequent chapters will dive deeper into specific algorithm families and their implementation in production pipelines.

Chapter 19: Feature Engineering with Graph-Based Metrics

In machine learning, the performance of a model is often determined less by the choice of algorithm and more by the quality and relevance of the features used. Graph databases, like Amazon Neptune Analytics, open a new frontier in **feature engineering** by enabling developers and ML practitioners to extract highly informative **structural and relational features** that represent complex, real-world relationships.

This chapter focuses on **feature engineering from graph data** using Neptune Analytics. We'll cover techniques for generating features using native algorithms, query patterns, and vector operations, enabling you to integrate graph-derived insights into your AI/ML pipelines.

Why Use Graph Features?

Graph-based features capture relationships, influence, communities, and proximity—characteristics that flat tabular data often misses. For example:

- **Centrality** indicates importance or influence.

- **Connectivity** suggests behavioral similarity.

- **Community membership** implies shared traits.

- **Vector embeddings** reflect semantic or structural similarity.

These features can improve models for:

- Fraud detection (who interacts unusually often?)

- Recommendation systems (who is similar or connected?)

- Churn prediction (who's central in a retention-prone group?)

- Entity resolution (are these two nodes essentially the same?)

Types of Graph-Based Features

Neptune Analytics supports a wide range of graph metrics you can use for feature engineering:

Feature Type	Algorithm / Query	Use Case
Node Centrality	`.pageRank()`, `.closenessCentrality()`	Influence, importance scoring
Edge Weights	`.jaccardSimilarity()`, `.overlapSimilarity()`	Link prediction, similarity

Communit y Detection	`.labelPropagation( ), .wcc()`	Customer segmentation, fraud rings
Proximity	`.sssp()` (shortest paths), `.bfs()`	Distance-aware scoring
Structural Embeddin gs	`.vectors.upsert()` + `.topKByEmbedding()`	Recommendati ons, vector search
Graph Topology Queries	openCypher (e.g. degree, neighbors)	Rule-based features

Architecture: Generating Graph Features with Neptune Analytics

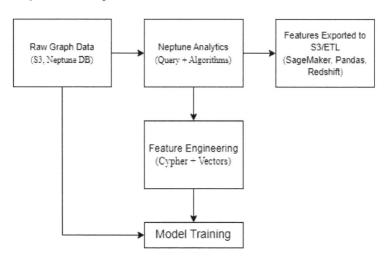

You can perform feature extraction in-place (using Neptune Analytics APIs), and then use the results in:

- SageMaker training pipelines.

- Real-time scoring services.

- Analytical dashboards in QuickSight or Athena.

Feature Engineering Recipes

1. Degree Features

The number of edges a node has—simple, yet powerful.

```
MATCH (n)
RETURN id(n) AS node_id, size((n)--()) AS degree
```

Use as a feature: user_connection_count

2. PageRank: Influence Score

185

```
CALL algo.pageRank()
YIELD nodeId, score
RETURN nodeId, score
```

Feature: `pagerank_score`

Can be scaled or normalized for ML models. Useful in recommender systems or leader detection.

---

3. Closeness Centrality: Accessibility

```
CALL algo.closenessCentrality()
YIELD nodeId, score
RETURN nodeId, score
```

Feature: `closeness_score`

Higher values suggest the node is topologically "close" to others—useful for information spread or risk analysis.

---

4. Community Features via Label Propagation

```
CALL algo.labelPropagation()
YIELD nodeId, communityId
```

```
RETURN nodeId, communityId
```

Feature: `community_id`

Helps ML models cluster similar behavior or attributes together.

---

5. Similarity Features: Jaccard Coefficient

```
CALL algo.jaccardSimilarity()
YIELD node1, node2, score
RETURN node1, node2, score
```

Feature: `similarity_to_target`

You can pivot this feature to capture similarity between users, products, or any pairwise entity.

---

6. Shortest Path Length to Important Nodes

For example, calculate distance to a known "high risk" node:

```
MATCH (start {~id: "user123"}), (target
{risk: "high"})
CALL algo.sssp(start, target)
YIELD distance
```

```
RETURN distance
```

Feature: `distance_to_high_risk`

Great for fraud detection or influence analysis.

---

7. Vector-Based Embeddings for ML

Graph embeddings represent nodes in high-dimensional space based on their structural context.

- Load embeddings:

```
CALL algo.vectors.upsert({
  nodeId: "product123",
  embedding: [0.12, 0.43, 0.33, ...]
})
```

- Retrieve similar nodes:

```
CALL algo.vectors.topKByEmbedding({
  embedding: [...],
  k: 5
})
YIELD nodeId, score
```

Feature: `top_k_similar_embeddings`

These vectors can be exported and used in deep learning models, especially recommender systems or GenAI contexts.

Exporting Engineered Features

Once you've engineered features inside Neptune Analytics, use the CLI or SDK to export for modeling:

```
aws neptune-graph start-export-task \
   --graph-identifier g-12345678 \
   --format CSV \
   --output-location s3://my-ml-features-bucket/features/
```

Or query and capture results directly:

```
import boto3
client = boto3.client("neptune-graph")

resp = client.execute_query(
    graphIdentifier="g-12345678",
```

```
    queryString="MATCH (n) RETURN id(n),
size((n)--()) AS degree",
    language="OPEN_CYPHER"
)


print(resp['payload'].read().decode('utf-
8'))
```

Best Practices for Graph Feature Engineering

- **Avoid overfitting with leakage**: If label-based
  features (e.g., distance to fraud) are used, ensure
  they're not from future data.

- **Normalize or bucket features**: Graph scores
  often span wide ranges (e.g., PageRank), which
  need scaling for model input.

- **Use meaningful identifiers**: Ensure ~id or
  custom IDs are consistent across systems.

- **Join features outside Neptune when needed**:
  Use S3 and Athena or Pandas to join graph
  features with tabular sources.

Real-World Use Case: Product Recommendations

190

In an ecommerce graph:

- Nodes: products, users, categories

- Edges: viewed, bought, added_to_cart

Features engineered:

- `pagerank_score` → Popularity

- `community_id` → Co-purchase clusters

- `similarity_to_target_product` → Jaccard similarity

- `user_embedding` → Learned from past behaviors

These features fed into a SageMaker XGBoost model to rank recommendations.

Summary

Graph feature engineering expands the ML toolbox with rich, relational signals that boost model accuracy, robustness, and explainability. Neptune Analytics offers a full stack for computing, storing, and exporting these features at cloud scale.

In this chapter, we explored a broad spectrum of graph-derived metrics—centrality, similarity, community detection, and embeddings—and how they can be used as features in modern AI/ML workflows.

Chapter 20: Recommender Systems with Community and Similarity Detection

Recommender systems have become foundational to user engagement across platforms—from e-commerce and streaming to social networks and enterprise productivity tools. Traditional recommendation engines often rely on collaborative filtering or content-based methods. However, these approaches can struggle to capture the nuanced relationships and communities that exist within user-item interaction data.

Enter **graph-based recommendation**, where **Neptune Analytics** shines by enabling community-aware and similarity-driven recommendations at massive scale. In this chapter, we'll explore how to build intelligent, graph-powered recommender systems using **community detection** and **similarity algorithms** natively supported in Amazon Neptune Analytics.

Why Graph-Based Recommendations?

Graphs naturally model:

- **User-item interactions** (e.g., *user viewed product*)

- **Social or behavioral links** (e.g., *user follows user*)

- **Hierarchies and categories** (e.g., *product belongs to category*)

These relationships can power:

- **Community-driven recommendations**: Suggest items from a user's cluster.

- **Similarity-based recommendations**: Recommend items similar to previously liked ones.

- **Hybrid recommendations**: Combine multiple signals (e.g., similarity + popularity).

By leveraging **Neptune's in-memory analytics engine**, we can run these algorithms efficiently on large datasets and use the results for real-time or batch recommendation pipelines.

Graph Schema for Recommendations

Here's a typical property graph schema used for recommender systems:

```
(:User)-[:VIEWED|LIKED|BOUGHT]->(:Product)
(:Product)-[:SIMILAR_TO]->(:Product)
(:Product)-[:IN_CATEGORY]->(:Category)
```

- Nodes: User, Product, Category

- Relationships: user interactions, item similarity, category hierarchy

Recommendation Strategy 1: Community Detection

Community detection groups users or items into **clusters** based on their connections. Users within the same cluster tend to have similar preferences.

Neptune Algorithm: `.labelPropagation()`

```
CALL algo.labelPropagation()
YIELD nodeId, communityId
RETURN nodeId, communityId
```

Once community IDs are assigned, you can recommend popular items within a user's community.

```
// Get community of a specific user
MATCH (u:User {~id: "user123"})
CALL algo.labelPropagation()
YIELD nodeId, communityId
WITH communityId
// Recommend top products bought by this
community
MATCH (u:User)-[:BOUGHT]->(p:Product)
WHERE u.communityId = communityId
RETURN p, COUNT(*) AS popularity
ORDER BY popularity DESC
```

195

```
LIMIT 10
```

Use Case:

- Recommend trending items in a user's social or behavioral circle.

- Cold-start scenarios for new users with minimal activity.

Recommendation Strategy 2: Item Similarity (Jaccard / Overlap)

Similarity-based recommendations find items **structurally close** in the graph—e.g., items frequently co-viewed or co-purchased.

Neptune Algorithms:

- `.jaccardSimilarity()`

- `.overlapSimilarity()`

These work best in a **user-item bipartite graph**.

```
CALL algo.jaccardSimilarity()
YIELD node1, node2, score
RETURN node1, node2, score
```

```
ORDER BY score DESC
LIMIT 100
```

Example: Recommend similar products to a product a
user just viewed:

```
MATCH (p:Product {~id: "product123"})
CALL algo.jaccardSimilarity()
YIELD node1, node2, score
WHERE node1 = p OR node2 = p
WITH CASE WHEN node1 = p THEN node2 ELSE
node1 END AS recommendedProduct, score
RETURN recommendedProduct, score
ORDER BY score DESC
LIMIT 5
```

Use Case:

- Show similar products below a product page.

- Complementary item suggestions during checkout.

Recommendation Strategy 3: Hybrid Recommendations

Combine **community detection** and **item similarity** for more personalized suggestions.

```
// Find user community
MATCH (u:User {~id: "user123"})
CALL algo.labelPropagation()
YIELD nodeId, communityId
WITH communityId


// Recommend products frequently bought in
that community
MATCH (u:User)-[:BOUGHT]->(p:Product)
WHERE u.communityId = communityId
WITH p, COUNT(*) AS score


// Find similar items to those the user
viewed
MATCH (u:User {~id: "user123"})-[:VIEWED]-
>(v:Product)
CALL algo.jaccardSimilarity()
YIELD node1, node2, score AS simScore
WHERE node1 = v OR node2 = v
WITH CASE WHEN node1 = v THEN node2 ELSE
node1 END AS simProduct, simScore


// Merge signals
MATCH (p:Product)
```

```
WHERE p = simProduct
RETURN p, score + simScore AS finalScore
ORDER BY finalScore DESC
LIMIT 10
```

Use Case:

- Personalized homepage or daily recommendation emails.

- Re-engagement campaigns based on both behavior and interest groups.

Scaling and Exporting Recommendations

To use these insights outside Neptune, export the results to Amazon S3:

```
aws neptune-graph start-export-task \
  --graph-identifier g-456def \
  --format CSV \
  --output-location s3://recommendation-data/output/
```

Or execute and stream results in real time via SDK:

```python
import boto3

client = boto3.client("neptune-graph")

response = client.execute_query(
    graphIdentifier='g-456def',
    queryString='MATCH (u:User)-[:BOUGHT]-
>(p:Product) RETURN u, p',
    language='OPEN_CYPHER'
)
print(response['payload'].read().decode('u
tf-8'))
```

Best Practices for Graph Recommendations

- **Precompute similarity indexes**: Run Jaccard or label propagation periodically, store results as new edges (`:SIMILAR_TO`).

- **Combine multiple edge types**: Consider different types of interactions (e.g., `VIEWED`, `LIKED`, `BOUGHT`) for a richer graph.

- **Weight interactions**: You can weight similarity or centrality based on recency or frequency.

- **Use vector embeddings**: Neptune supports loading learned embeddings for vector search (see Chapter 21).

Real-World Example: Video Streaming App

In a streaming app:

- Nodes: users, videos, genres

- Edges: viewed, liked, rated, belongs_to

Recommendations powered by:

- `.labelPropagation()` → user clusters by genre preferences

- `.jaccardSimilarity()` → related videos

- `.vectors.topKByEmbedding()` → embedding-based video similarity

Combined in a hybrid model to drive personalized feeds and "You Might Also Like" sections.

Visualizing Recommendations

Neptune Analytics supports Jupyter-based graph notebooks for exploration:

```
%%oc
```

```
MATCH (u:User {~id: "user123"})-[:BOUGHT]-
>(p:Product)
RETURN u, p
```

Or use `%summary`, `%seed`, and
`%%graph_notebook_vis_options` for interactive
visualizations.

Summary

Graph-based recommender systems offer a new level of
precision by understanding **who users are connected to**,
what communities they belong to, and **how their
behaviors relate** to others. Neptune Analytics provides
built-in algorithms, in-memory performance, and easy
AWS integration to support real-time and batch
recommendation at scale.

This chapter covered how to use **community detection**
and **similarity algorithms** to power effective
recommendations, including hybrid approaches that unify
user-centric and item-centric signals.

Chapter 21: Fraud Detection Using Graph Patterns

Fraud detection is a high-stakes use case where success hinges on identifying complex, hidden relationships across vast volumes of data. Traditional rule-based systems and flat ML models often fall short in catching coordinated fraud, account takeovers, or money laundering due to their inability to detect relational and temporal patterns.

In this chapter, we explore how **Amazon Neptune Analytics** enables **graph-based fraud detection** by uncovering suspicious patterns, relationships, and behaviors at scale. We'll walk through practical detection strategies using **graph queries**, **topological algorithms**, and **vector analysis** to build a graph-native fraud detection engine.

Why Use Graphs for Fraud Detection?

Fraud is rarely isolated—it thrives in relationships. Graphs allow you to:

- Model **real-world entities and connections**: users, accounts, IPs, devices, transactions.

- Detect **ring structures, collusion, and shared identifiers**.

- Score nodes by **centrality, proximity to fraud, or behavioral similarity**.

- Run **continuous detection queries** and **batch analytics** for investigations.

Neptune Analytics' in-memory processing, graph algorithms, and Cypher query capabilities make it an ideal platform for near real-time or batch fraud analytics.

Fraud Graph Data Model

A typical fraud detection graph may include:

```
(:User)-[:LOGGED_IN_FROM]->(:IP)
(:User)-[:USES]->(:Device)
(:User)-[:OWNS]->(:Account)
(:Account)-[:TRANSFERS_TO]->(:Account)
(:User)-[:REFERRED]->(:User)
(:Account)-[:FLAGGED_AS]->(:Fraud)
```

This schema helps identify suspicious activities such as:

- Multiple users using the same IP or device.

- High-volume transfers between tightly connected accounts.

- Accounts connected to known fraud cases.

Strategy 1: Ring Detection Using Weakly Connected Components (WCC)

Fraud rings often form tight clusters of accounts or users. WCC groups nodes that are connected, directly or indirectly.

```
CALL algo.wcc()
YIELD componentId, nodeId
RETURN componentId, COUNT(*) AS size
ORDER BY size DESC
LIMIT 10
```

> Feature: `component_size`, used to detect tightly linked clusters.

To isolate large suspicious clusters:

```
CALL algo.wcc()
YIELD componentId, nodeId
WITH componentId, COUNT(*) AS size
WHERE size > 5
MATCH (a)-[*1..3]-(b)
WHERE a.componentId = componentId AND
b.componentId = componentId
RETURN a, b
```

Strategy 2: Shared Identifiers Detection

Fraudsters reuse IP addresses, devices, or emails to control multiple accounts.

```
MATCH (u1:User)-[:USES]->(d:Device)<-
[:USES]-(u2:User)
WHERE u1 <> u2
RETURN u1, u2, d
```

Filter by frequency to detect overused identifiers:

```
MATCH (d:Device)<-[:USES]-(u:User)
WITH d, COUNT(DISTINCT u) AS userCount
WHERE userCount > 5
RETURN d, userCount
```

Strategy 3: Proximity to Known Fraud

Use shortest path algorithms to assess risk by proximity to known fraudulent accounts.

```
MATCH (a:Account {~id: "targetAccount"}),
(f:Fraud)
CALL algo.sssp(a, f)
```

206

```
YIELD distance
RETURN distance
```

> Feature: `distance_to_fraud` — smaller
> distance increases suspicion.

This can be applied in batch to all active accounts:

```
MATCH (a:Account), (f:Fraud)
CALL algo.sssp(a, f)
YIELD nodeId, distance
RETURN nodeId, MIN(distance) AS
min_distance
```

Strategy 4: Centrality Analysis for Influence Detection

Identify key accounts or users coordinating many others.

Use **PageRank** to find nodes that receive many connections from important nodes:

```
CALL algo.pageRank()
YIELD nodeId, score
RETURN nodeId, score
ORDER BY score DESC
```

Feature: `pagerank_score` — high scores can indicate brokers or mule accounts.

Strategy 5: Similarity Analysis for Behavior-Based Clustering

Fraudsters may mimic the structure of legitimate accounts. Similarity algorithms can detect clusters of nearly identical behavior.

Jaccard Similarity:

```
CALL algo.jaccardSimilarity()
YIELD node1, node2, score
WHERE score > 0.8
RETURN node1, node2, score
```

Find similar accounts to known fraud:

```
MATCH (f:Account)-[:FLAGGED_AS]->(:Fraud)
CALL algo.jaccardSimilarity()
YIELD node1, node2, score
WHERE node1 = f AND score > 0.75
RETURN node2 AS suspiciousAccount, score
```

Strategy 6: Fraud Embeddings with Vector Similarity

For deep-learning-based behavior modeling, you can load vector embeddings and use vector search to find similar fraud patterns.

Upsert embeddings:

```
CALL algo.vectors.upsert({
  nodeId: "acct123",
  embedding: [0.23, 0.56, 0.12, ...]
})
```

Find top-k similar nodes:

```
CALL algo.vectors.topKByEmbedding({
  embedding: [0.23, 0.56, 0.12, ...],
  k: 5
})
YIELD nodeId, score
RETURN nodeId, score
```

These methods power anomaly detection based on structural and behavioral embeddings.

Building a Real-Time Fraud Scoring Engine

You can implement a scoring system combining the above metrics:

Feature Name	Description
pagerank_score	Centrality of user/account
component_size	Size of connected fraud ring
shared_identifier	Reuse of IP/device/email
distance_to_fraud	Proximity to flagged fraud nodes
similarity_to_fraud	Jaccard or vector similarity

Sample Query Combining Features:

```
MATCH (a:Account)
OPTIONAL MATCH (a)-[:USES]->(d:Device)
WITH a, COUNT(DISTINCT d) AS devices_used

CALL algo.pageRank()
YIELD nodeId, score AS pagerank

CALL algo.jaccardSimilarity()
YIELD node1, node2, score
WHERE node1 = a AND node2:Fraud
```

```
RETURN a, pagerank, devices_used, score AS
similarity_to_fraud
ORDER BY similarity_to_fraud DESC
```

Export features to S3 for modeling:

```
aws neptune-graph start-export-task \
  --graph-identifier g-fraud-graph \
  --format CSV \
  --output-location s3://fraud-
features/export/
```

Monitoring and Investigation with Notebooks

Use **Jupyter notebooks + Neptune graph-notebook** for:

- Visualizing fraud rings.

- Tracing relationships interactively.

- Testing ad-hoc hypotheses via %oc magic queries.

Example:

```
%%oc
MATCH path = (f:Fraud)-[*1..3]-(a:Account)
```

Best Practices

- **Periodically recompute algorithms** (e.g., WCC, PageRank) to adapt to graph changes.

- **Precompute suspicious edges** like :SIMILAR_TO, :LIKELY_FRAUD.

- **Enrich graph with external signals**: geolocation, timestamps, flags.

- **Combine real-time and batch pipelines** using AWS Lambda + Neptune Analytics.

Real-World Use Case: Fintech Payment Network

- Fraudsters use multiple accounts with shared devices to perform fraudulent transfers.

- Neptune Analytics detected clusters via .wcc() and ranked risky accounts via .pageRank().

- Investigators used notebooks to visualize rings.

- Embedded fraud signals powered real-time scoring APIs in Lambda functions.

Summary

Fraud detection is one of the most compelling use cases for graph analytics. With Neptune Analytics, you can:

- Model complex fraud relationships.

- Run scalable, in-memory algorithms to detect suspicious structures.

- Extract meaningful features for scoring and investigations.

- Visualize and explain results interactively.

This chapter has shown how to design graph-based fraud detection workflows using Neptune's native capabilities— from ring detection to similarity analysis and beyond.

Chapter 22: Building Knowledge Graphs for NLP

Natural Language Processing (NLP) has evolved beyond simple keyword matching and syntactic parsing. To truly **understand, reason, and generate** human-like responses, AI systems must contextualize language in the real world. This is where **knowledge graphs (KGs)** shine—linking entities, relationships, and facts into structured, queryable formats that enhance comprehension.

Amazon Neptune Analytics provides a high-performance, scalable platform for **building and analyzing knowledge graphs**, especially for **text-centric AI workflows** such as:

- Document classification

- Semantic search

- Question answering (QA)

- Retrieval-augmented generation (RAG)

In this chapter, we explore how to extract, construct, and leverage **knowledge graphs from unstructured text** using Neptune Analytics as the graph engine in your NLP architecture.

What is a Knowledge Graph?

A **Knowledge Graph** is a graph-based representation of **entities** (people, places, events, concepts) and their **relationships**. It typically follows the format:

```
(Entity A) -[Relationship]- (Entity B)
```

For example:

```
(Ada Lovelace) -[INVENTED]- (Analytical
Engine)
(Paris) -[IS_CAPITAL_OF] . (France)
```

Knowledge graphs can be derived from structured data or **extracted from natural language** using NLP techniques like Named Entity Recognition (NER), Dependency Parsing, and Relation Extraction.

Architecture: NLP-Driven Knowledge Graph with Neptune

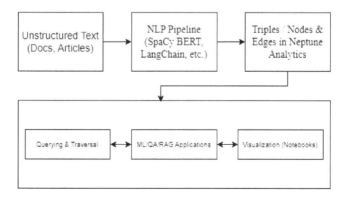

Step 1: Extracting Graph Data from Text

Use NLP libraries or LLMs to extract **entity-relation-entity (E-R-E)** triples.

Example (Python + SpaCy):

```python
import spacy
from spacy.matcher import Matcher

nlp = spacy.load("en_core_web_sm")
text = "Ada Lovelace invented the Analytical Engine in the 19th century."
doc = nlp(text)

for ent in doc.ents:
    print(ent.text, ent.label_)

# Output: Ada Lovelace (PERSON), Analytical Engine (PRODUCT)

# Create triple:
("Ada Lovelace", "INVENTED", "Analytical Engine")
```

More advanced pipelines can use **transformers** (e.g., BERT, OpenAI, Hugging Face) to extract custom relations using relation extraction models.

Alternatively, with LLMs (via LangChain or AWS Bedrock):

```
Prompt: Extract subject, relation, object
from the following:
"Ada Lovelace invented the Analytical
Engine."


Response: ("Ada Lovelace", "invented",
"Analytical Engine")
```

Step 2: Loading the Graph into Neptune Analytics

Once you have triples, format them into **CSV or RDF** and load them into Neptune.

Option A: Load using CSV

CSV Schema:

```
nodes.csv


~id,~label
ada_lovelace,Person
analytical_engine,Invention
```

```
edges.csv

~id,~from,~to,~label
invented_1,ada_lovelace,analytical_engine,
INVENTED
```

-

Bulk load into Neptune Analytics:

```
aws neptune-graph create-graph-using-
import-task \
  --graph-name "nlp-kg" \
  --region us-east-1 \
  --format "CSV" \
  --source "s3://my-nlp-bucket/knowledge-
graph/" \
  --role-arn
"arn:aws:iam::123456789012:role/GraphLoade
rRole" \
  --public-connectivity
```

Option B: Use Neptune Python SDK (boto3)

```
client = boto3.client("neptune-graph")
client.execute_query(
```

```
    graphIdentifier="nlp-kg",

    queryString="""

        CREATE (:Person {~id:
"ada_lovelace"})-[:INVENTED]->(:Invention
{~id: "analytical_engine"})

        """,

    language="OPEN_CYPHER"
)
```

Step 3: Enriching and Traversing the Knowledge Graph

Once loaded, you can run semantic queries:

Example 1: List all inventions by historical figures

```
MATCH (p:Person)-[:INVENTED]-
>(i:Invention)
RETURN p, i
```

Example 2: All entities related to "France"

```
MATCH (n)-[r]->(e {~id: "france"})
```

```
RETURN n, r, e
```

Example 3: Degree centrality for high-context nodes

```
MATCH (n)
RETURN id(n), size((n)--()) AS degree
ORDER BY degree DESC
LIMIT 10
```

These queries allow you to build applications such as:

- Intelligent document exploration

- Entity disambiguation tools

- Semantic search engines

Step 4: Powering NLP Applications

A. Question Answering (QA)

Use the KG as a backend for a knowledge-aware QA system:

```
MATCH (a:Person)-[:INVENTED]-
>(b:Invention)
```

```
WHERE a.name = "Ada Lovelace"
RETURN b.name
```

B. Semantic Search

Given a query like *"What machine did Ada Lovelace design?"*, parse the intent and query the graph.

You can also use **vector search** for fuzzy matching (see Chapter 21).

C. Retrieval-Augmented Generation (RAG)

Use Neptune + LLMs:

1. Retrieve relevant subgraphs from Neptune.

2. Pass results to the LLM prompt.

3. Generate answers grounded in structured knowledge.

Step 5: Visualizing Knowledge Graphs in Notebooks

Use **Neptune Workbench notebooks** to explore and visualize relationships:

```
%%oc
MATCH (p:Person)-[r]->(e)
RETURN p, r, e
```

Or view a graph summary:

```
%summary
```

Enable visualization controls:

```
%%graph_notebook_vis_options
{
  "node_color_property": "~label",
  "relationship_color_property": "~label"
}
```

Best Practices for Knowledge Graph NLP Workflows

- **Normalize entities** (e.g., synonyms, aliases) during extraction.

- **Deduplicate relationships** using consistent IDs.

- **Use custom relationship labels** to enhance semantic meaning (e.g., INVENTED, LOCATED_IN).

- **Combine structured and vector search** for hybrid NLP pipelines.

- **Use temporal attributes** (e.g., `year`, `timestamp`) for fact tracking.

Real-World Use Case: Legal Document Knowledge Graph

- **Input**: thousands of legal case documents.

- **Pipeline**:

    - Extract persons, organizations, laws referenced.

    - Connect citations across cases.

    - Identify clusters using `.wcc()` and `.labelPropagation()`.

- **Application**: Legal search assistant using QA over Neptune + LLM.

Summary

Knowledge graphs are becoming a key foundation for intelligent NLP systems. With Amazon Neptune Analytics, you can:

- Transform raw text into structured, queryable graph knowledge.

- Perform in-memory graph analytics to understand relationships.

- Power semantic search, question answering, and RAG workflows.

- Integrate graph and vector reasoning for hybrid AI systems.

This chapter provided a practical framework to build and leverage knowledge graphs for NLP using AWS-native tools and Neptune Analytics' powerful graph capabilities.

Chapter 23: Real-Time AI Inference via Neptune and Jupyter

Modern AI systems are increasingly required to **make decisions in real time**—from fraud detection at the moment of transaction, to generating dynamic recommendations as users interact with a platform. When these tasks depend on **rich relational data** and **fast inference**, Amazon Neptune Analytics and **Jupyter-based notebooks** provide a powerful solution.

This chapter shows how to build **real-time, graph-aware AI inference pipelines** using Neptune Analytics and Jupyter notebooks. We'll walk through the architecture, use cases, and techniques for integrating graph data, AI models, and interactive workflows in real time— empowering both automated systems and human-in-the-loop decision making.

Why Use Neptune and Jupyter for Real-Time AI?

Component	Role in Inference
Neptune Analytics	In-memory graph database with low-latency queries
Jupyter Notebooks	Interactive exploration and visualization of results
SageMaker / AI Models	Run ML models on graph-derived features
Neptune APIs/CLI	Execute queries in scripts or API layers

This combination enables:

- Live querying of graph features and relationships.

- Execution of AI inference in a human-interpretable workflow.

- Automation hooks for real-time use in APIs or Lambda functions.

- Visualization of AI decision context (e.g., subgraphs, centrality, embeddings).

Architecture: Real-Time Graph-Aware Inference

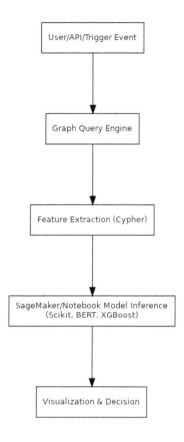

Step 1: Prepare the Graph in Neptune Analytics

Your graph should model relevant entities and events:

```
(:User)-[:VIEWED]->(:Product)
(:User)-[:OWNS]->(:Account)
(:Account)-[:TRANSFERRED_TO]->(:Account)
(:Account)-[:FLAGGED_AS]->(:Fraud)
```

Ensure:

- It is provisioned with public or private access.

- Your Jupyter notebook has credentials (IAM or role) to access the Neptune API.

- Vector search or analytic algorithms are enabled if needed.

Step 2: Set Up Your Jupyter Environment

Use one of the following:

- **Amazon SageMaker Notebook** (recommended for scalability and managed compute)

- **Local JupyterLab** (with `boto3` and `awscurl`)

- **Neptune Workbench** (graph-notebook with native Cypher magics)

Install necessary packages:

```
pip install boto3 pandas matplotlib
scikit-learn
```

Configure your notebook for Neptune:

```python
import boto3
from botocore.config import Config

config = Config(
    retries = {"total_max_attempts": 1},
    read_timeout = 0
)

client = boto3.client("neptune-graph",
config=config, region_name="us-east-1")
GRAPH_ID = "g-0123456789"
```

Step 3: Run Real-Time Graph Queries for Inference

Use openCypher queries to extract features from the
graph, based on a live input.

Example: Fetch Features for a Target User

```python
user_id = "user_123"
query = f"""
MATCH (u:User {{~id: "{user_id}"}})-
[:OWNS]->(a:Account)
OPTIONAL MATCH (a)-[:TRANSFERRED_TO]->(b)
WITH u, a, COUNT(b) AS transfer_count
```

```
RETURN id(u) AS user_id, id(a) AS
account_id, transfer_count
"""


response = client.execute_query(
    graphIdentifier=GRAPH_ID,
    queryString=query,
    language="OPEN_CYPHER"
)


import pandas as pd
import io
features =
pd.read_csv(io.BytesIO(response["payload"]
.read()))
features.head()
```

Step 4: Pass Graph Features into a Live AI Model

Assuming you've trained an ML model (e.g., XGBoost) on graph-derived features, load and run it:

```
import joblib
model = joblib.load("fraud_detector.pkl")
```

```
prediction =
model.predict(features[["transfer_count"]]
)
print("Fraud Likelihood:", prediction[0])
```

```
Or use an embedding for similarity:
```

```
query = """
CALL algo.vectors.topKByNode({
  nodeId: "user_123",
  k: 5
})
YIELD nodeId, score
RETURN nodeId, score
"""
```

Step 5: Visualize Real-Time Context in Jupyter

Use %%oc magic from the graph-notebook to display relationships:

```
%%oc
```

```
MATCH (u:User {~id: "user_123"})-[r*1..2]-
(x)
RETURN u, r, x
```

Enable visual themes:

```
%%graph_notebook_vis_options
{
  "node_color_property": "~label",
  "relationship_thickness_property":
"score"
}
```

Step 6: Automate via API or Lambda for Real-Time Triggering

Your notebook can prototype logic that's later moved to an event-driven system:

```
def get_graph_features(user_id):
    q = f"""
    MATCH (u:User {{~id: "{user_id}"}})-
[:OWNS]->(a:Account)
```

```
    OPTIONAL MATCH (a)-[:TRANSFERRED_TO]-
>(b)

    RETURN COUNT(b) AS transfer_count
    """

    r =
client.execute_query(graphIdentifier=GRAPH
_ID, queryString=q,
language="OPEN_CYPHER")

    df =
pd.read_csv(io.BytesIO(r["payload"].read()
))

    return df["transfer_count"][0]
```

Deploy this into an AWS Lambda function that's triggered via:

- New transactions

- User login

- Alerting systems

Use Cases

Use Case	Real-Time Graph-Aware Logic
Fraud detection	Check centrality, recent behavior, connected fraud rings

Dynamic recommendation	Recommend products connected to current session activity
Access control	Verify relationships before allowing access (e.g., org chart graphs)
Incident response (SOC)	Map threat propagation from a compromised endpoint
GenAI Retrieval	Retrieve related subgraphs for LLM grounding

Best Practices

- **Use in-memory algorithms sparingly in real time** (precompute and cache where possible).

- **Limit traversal depth in live queries** ($*1..2$ instead of deep unbounded paths).

- **Secure your notebook and Neptune graph** using IAM roles and private endpoints.

- **Log and store query traces** for audit and refinement.

- **Validate inputs**: never pass user input directly into queries without sanitization.

Real-World Example: Real-Time KYC (Know Your Customer)

A fintech platform uses Neptune to:

234

- Model relationships between users, accounts, referrals, and locations.

- In real time, fetch graph-based risk scores during onboarding.

- Trigger deeper document verification if graph signals exceed thresholds.

The entire workflow is prototyped in Jupyter notebooks and later deployed as microservices using AWS Lambda, Neptune Analytics, and SageMaker.

Summary

Neptune Analytics and Jupyter Notebooks form a dynamic duo for real-time, graph-powered AI inference. Whether you're detecting fraud, making recommendations, or enriching LLMs with live knowledge, this architecture supports:

- Interactive prototyping and exploration

- Low-latency, graph-based decision making

- Seamless integration with AWS AI/ML stack

By combining **graph context** with **AI inference**, developers and ML engineers can deliver intelligent, explainable, and scalable real-time systems.

Part V – In-Memory & Search Databases for AI/ML

Chapter 24: Implementing Vector Search and Semantic Caching

Amazon MemoryDB has evolved beyond traditional in-memory key-value stores by introducing **native vector search** capabilities. These capabilities, combined with **semantic caching**, make MemoryDB a compelling choice for AI/ML workloads, particularly those involving **Retrieval-Augmented Generation (RAG)**, **embedding search**, and **intelligent real-time applications**.

This chapter explores how to implement vector search and semantic caching using MemoryDB, including architecture, commands, integration with machine learning workflows, and best practices for performance and scalability.

Introduction to Vector Search in MemoryDB

Vector search allows you to store and query **vector embeddings** directly in MemoryDB, enabling fast similarity lookups that are crucial for:

- **Semantic search**

- **Recommendation systems**

- **Anomaly detection**

- **Fraud detection**

- **Chatbot memory for LLMs (e.g., RAG)**

Core Concepts

- **Vector indexes** are created with the `FT.CREATE` command.

- MemoryDB uses the **HNSW (Hierarchical Navigable Small World)** algorithm for approximate nearest neighbor (ANN) search.

- You can store vectors alongside structured metadata (e.g., tags, timestamps).

Enabling Vector Search in a MemoryDB Cluster

To enable vector search, you must create the cluster with specific settings:

```
aws memorydb create-cluster \
  --cluster-name rag-cluster \
  --node-type db.r6g.large \
  --engine valkey \
  --engine-version 7.2 \
  --shards 1 \
  --replicas-per-shard 1 \
  --acl-name my-acl \
  --subnet-group my-subnet-group \
```

```
--parameter-group-name default.memorydb-
valkey7.search \
  --tls-enabled
```

> **Note:** Vector search requires Valkey 7.2.6+
> and a specific parameter group configured for
> vector operations.

Creating a Vector Index

Example: Storing Embeddings for Semantic Search

```
FT.CREATE vector_index ON HASH PREFIX 1
doc: SCHEMA
  title TEXT
  content TEXT
  embedding VECTOR HNSW 6 TYPE FLOAT32 DIM
768 DISTANCE_METRIC COSINE
```

This index creates a hybrid search schema:

- title, content: for full-text search

- embedding: for similarity-based vector search
  using HNSW

239

Ingesting Embeddings

Python Example with `redis-py`

```python
import redis
import numpy as np

client = redis.Redis(
    host='your-cluster-endpoint',
    port=6379,
    password='your-password',
    ssl=True
)

# Simulate a vector embedding
embedding =
np.random.rand(768).astype(np.float32).tob
ytes()

client.hset("doc:123", mapping={
    "title": "MemoryDB for AI",
    "content": "A guide to vector search
and caching in MemoryDB.",
    "embedding": embedding
})
```

> Tip: Store embeddings using `FLOAT32` with
> proper byte encoding (`tobytes()`) to avoid
> serialization errors.

```
FT.SEARCH vector_index "*=>[KNN 5
@embedding $vec_param]" PARAMS 2 vec_param
"$BINARY_VECTOR" DIALECT 2
```

Python Example

```
query_vector =
np.random.rand(768).astype(np.float32).tob
ytes()

results =
client.ft("vector_index").search(
    Query("*=>[KNN 5 @embedding
$vec]").dialect(2).params({"vec":
query_vector})
)
```

Building a Semantic Cache for AI/ML

Semantic caching stores embeddings and responses from an LLM or ML model so that **similar queries can reuse past results** instead of invoking expensive models.

Workflow

1. Generate embedding from query using a model like `sentence-transformers`.

2. Use FT.SEARCH with vector query to find similar past queries.

3. If similarity > threshold, return cached result.

4. Otherwise, invoke model and cache the result.

Schema Design

```
FT.CREATE semantic_cache ON HASH PREFIX 1
cache: SCHEMA
  query TEXT
  response TEXT
  embedding VECTOR HNSW 6 TYPE FLOAT32 DIM
768 DISTANCE_METRIC COSINE
```

Retrieval-Augmented Generation (RAG) Pattern

MemoryDB can act as the **retriever** in RAG systems.

Architecture Diagram (Text)

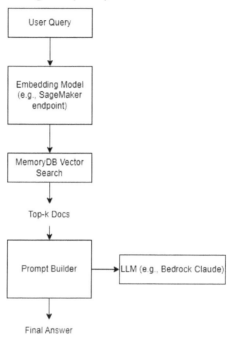

Benefits of MemoryDB in RAG

- Ultra-fast retrieval (<10ms)

- Durable in-memory store

- Easily integrates with SageMaker, Bedrock, Lambda

Best Practices for Vector Search in MemoryDB

Performance

- Use optimized HNSW parameters for your workload (M, EF_CONSTRUCTION, EF_RUNTIME)

- Keep embedding dimensions consistent

- Normalize embeddings if using cosine similarity

Durability and Scaling

- Always enable **Multi-AZ** with replicas for high availability

- Monitor `UsedMemoryDataset` and `memory_overhead` via CloudWatch

- Use **data tiering** (r6gd instances) for larger datasets

Security

- Use **TLS for in-transit encryption**

- Use **ACLs** to restrict command access (e.g., prevent `FT.DROPINDEX`)

- Audit queries with **CloudTrail**

Limitations and Considerations

- Vectors must be stored as `FLOAT32` binary

- No support yet for live updates of index parameters (must drop and recreate index)

- Currently limited to HNSW algorithm

Refer to the MemoryDB Vector Search Limits for the latest capacity and scaling guidelines.

Summary

MemoryDB's vector search and semantic caching capabilities unlock new possibilities for intelligent applications. By integrating fast, in-memory similarity search with structured metadata and ML model outputs, developers can:

- Reduce inference costs

- Improve response times

- Enable intelligent, real-time decision making

MemoryDB becomes not just a cache or a data store, but a **core intelligence layer** in modern AI/ML architectures.

Chapter 25: Retrieval-Augmented Generation (RAG) with MemoryDB

Retrieval-Augmented Generation (RAG) is a powerful architectural pattern that combines a large language model (LLM) with a high-speed knowledge retriever. Amazon MemoryDB is purpose-built to serve as the in-memory, low-latency, and durable vector retriever in this pipeline. In this chapter, you'll learn how to build an end-to-end RAG system using MemoryDB, from data ingestion to semantic search, and how to integrate it with LLMs via Amazon Bedrock, SageMaker, or third-party APIs.

What is Retrieval-Augmented Generation (RAG)?

RAG augments LLM responses by retrieving relevant context from external knowledge sources and passing that context along with the user query to the model.

Workflow Overview:

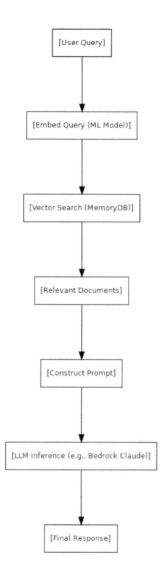

```
[User Query]
    |
    v
[Embed Query (ML Model)]
    |
    v
[Vector Search (MemoryDB)]
    |
    v
[Relevant Documents]
    |
    v
[Construct Prompt]
    |
    v
[LLM Inference (e.g., Bedrock Claude)]
    |
    v
[Final Response]
```

Why MemoryDB for RAG?

MemoryDB is an ideal fit for the retriever in a RAG
pipeline because it provides:

247

- **Microsecond-level read latency** (enables sub-100ms end-to-end responses)

- **Durable in-memory storage**, unlike traditional caches

- **Native vector search** via FT.CREATE, FT.SEARCH (Valkey)

- **Multi-AZ high availability**

- **Compatibility with Valkey and Redis OSS clients**

Architecture for RAG with MemoryDB

System Components

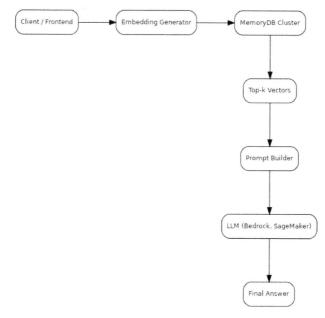

Setting Up MemoryDB for Vector Retrieval

Create a MemoryDB Cluster with Vector Search

```
aws memorydb create-cluster \
  --cluster-name rag-cluster \
  --node-type db.r6g.large \
  --engine valkey \
  --engine-version 7.2 \
  --shards 1 \
  --replicas-per-shard 1 \
```

```
  --acl-name rag-acl \
  --subnet-group rag-subnet-group \
  --parameter-group-name default.memorydb-
valkey7.search \
  --tls-enabled
```

Define Vector Index for Document Store

```
FT.CREATE docs ON HASH PREFIX 1 doc:
SCHEMA
  title TEXT
  content TEXT
  embedding VECTOR HNSW 6 TYPE FLOAT32 DIM
768 DISTANCE_METRIC COSINE
```

Ingesting Documents with Embeddings

Example: Python with `redis-py` **and** `sentence-transformers`

```
import redis
import numpy as np
from sentence_transformers import
SentenceTransformer

client = redis.Redis(
    host='your-endpoint',
    port=6379,
    password='your-password',
```

```
    ssl=True
)

model = SentenceTransformer("all-MiniLM-
L6-v2")

def store_document(doc_id, title,
content):
    embedding =
model.encode(content).astype(np.float32).t
obytes()
    client.hset(f"doc:{doc_id}", mapping={
        "title": title,
        "content": content,
        "embedding": embedding
    })

store_document("1", "What is MemoryDB?",
"Amazon MemoryDB is a Redis-compatible in-
memory database service.")
```

Semantic Retrieval for Query Augmentation

Embed and Query

```
query = "How does MemoryDB support RAG?"
```

```
query_vec =
model.encode(query).astype(np.float32).tob
ytes()

res = client.execute_command(
    "FT.SEARCH", "docs", "*=>[KNN 5
@embedding $vec_param]",
    "PARAMS", 2, "vec_param", query_vec,
    "DIALECT", 2
)
```

Construct Prompt

```
docs = [res[i+1]['content'] for i in
range(1, len(res), 2)]
context = "\n".join(docs)
prompt =
f"Context:\n{context}\n\nQuestion:\n{query
}\nAnswer:"
```

Passing to LLM for Final Generation

Using Amazon Bedrock

```
import boto3

bedrock = boto3.client("bedrock-runtime")
response = bedrock.invoke_model(
```

```
    modelId="anthropic.claude-v2",
    body=json.dumps({"prompt": prompt,
"max_tokens_to_sample": 300})
)
```

Caching Responses with MemoryDB

To prevent redundant LLM calls, cache question embeddings and generated responses.

```
client.hset(f"cache:{query_hash}",
mapping={
    "query": query,
    "response": llm_response,
    "embedding": query_vec
})
```

You can check semantic similarity between the incoming query and cached entries before generating again.

Scaling and Operations

Best Practices

- Enable **Multi-AZ** for fault tolerance

- Use **CloudWatch** to monitor memory and CPU

- Use **Redis Cluster clients** to automatically route requests across shards

- Scale shards horizontally to increase write throughput

- Max vectors per index: 1 billion (soft limit)

- Embedding type: `FLOAT32`, size must match `DIM`

- Max dimensions: 2048

- Use **TLS for all connections**

- Authenticate with **ACLs**

- Limit vector search commands to specific roles (e.g., disallow `FT.DROPINDEX` in prod)

- Audit with **CloudTrail**

```python
# Handler for a Lambda function triggered
by API Gateway
def handler(event, context):
    query = event["query"]
    query_vec =
model.encode(query).astype(np.float32).tob
ytes()

    # Search vector index in MemoryDB
    results = search_memorydb(query_vec)

    # Construct prompt from results
    prompt = build_prompt(query, results)

    # Generate response via LLM
    response = call_llm(prompt)

    return {"response": response}
```

Real-World Use Cases

Use Case	How RAG + MemoryDB Helps
Customer Support	Retrieve product manuals and policies instantly
Medical Assistant	Pull relevant case studies before LLM answer
Financial Services	Retrieve recent filings or regulatory docs

E-commerce	Recommend similar products using vector search
Legal Automation	Fetch precedents and statutes in prompts

Summary

By combining MemoryDB with a vector embedding model and an LLM, developers can create low-latency, intelligent, and context-aware applications. With built-in durability, scalability, and Valkey/Redis compatibility, MemoryDB simplifies the architecture of RAG systems while improving response times and cost-efficiency.

MemoryDB turns RAG from a research pattern into a production-ready capability for AWS-native AI applications.

Chapter 26: Cluster Design, Scaling, and Security for ML Apps

In AI/ML applications, the database layer must deliver **real-time access**, **low latency**, **horizontal scalability**, and **enterprise-grade security**. Amazon MemoryDB is purpose-built to meet these demands. As a durable, Redis-compatible in-memory database, MemoryDB combines microsecond-level read latency with multi-AZ high availability, making it ideal for ML inference, feature storage, vector search, and real-time model orchestration.

This chapter covers how to design, scale, and secure MemoryDB clusters for machine learning workloads, with implementation-ready guidance and AWS best practices.

Principles of Cluster Design for ML Use Cases

Key Workload Patterns

Pattern	Description
Real-time feature store	Stores features for online models
Model inference orchestration	Tracks input/output across microservices
Vector search / RAG	Embedding-based document retrieval
Semantic cache	Stores responses from LLMs for reuse

Each of these requires a **highly available**, **low-latency**, and **scalable** database that can process tens of millions of TPS.

Designing MemoryDB Clusters for ML Workloads

Choosing Cluster Parameters

When designing a MemoryDB cluster, consider:

- **Engine**: Use `valkey` (recommended) for full feature support and future compatibility.

- **Node Type**: Use `r6g` or `r7g` families for Graviton2/3 performance and cost-efficiency.

- **Shards**: Scale write throughput by increasing shards (horizontal partitioning).

- **Replicas**: Add replicas per shard for read scaling and HA.

- **Subnet Group**: Choose subnets in **at least 2 AZs** to ensure failover capability.

Example: CLI Command to Create a Cluster

```
aws memorydb create-cluster \
  --cluster-name ml-prod-cluster \
  --node-type db.r6g.2xlarge \
  --engine valkey \
```

```
--shards 4 \
--replicas-per-shard 1 \
--acl-name ml-acl \
--subnet-group ml-subnets \
--parameter-group-name default.memorydb-
valkey7 \
--tls-enabled
```

Scaling for Machine Learning Applications

Horizontal Scaling

MemoryDB supports:

- **Sharding** to scale write throughput

- **Replicas per shard** to scale read throughput and failover

You can scale dynamically using:

```
aws memorydb update-cluster \
  --cluster-name ml-prod-cluster \
  --shards 6 \
  --replicas-per-shard 2
```

> ⚠ Ensure your VPC subnet groups have sufficient IP capacity for scaling nodes.

Vertical Scaling

Change the node type (e.g., from `r6g.large` to `r6g.4xlarge`) for more memory and CPU.

```
aws memorydb update-cluster \
  --cluster-name ml-prod-cluster \
  --node-type db.r6g.4xlarge
```

Note: Vertical scaling requires node replacement and may cause brief failover events.

Auto Scaling

MemoryDB does not offer native auto scaling, but you can implement it using:

- Amazon CloudWatch (for memory/CPU thresholds)

- AWS Lambda (trigger updates)

- Step Functions or EventBridge for orchestration

Security Design for ML Applications

MemoryDB offers multiple layers of security:

IAM for Administrative Access

Use IAM policies for API-level access control.

```
{
  "Effect": "Allow",
  "Action": [
    "memorydb:CreateCluster",
    "memorydb:TagResource"
  ],
  "Resource": "*"
}
```

☑ Best Practice: Assign least-privilege roles to dev/test/staging environments.

Access Control Lists (ACLs) for Data Access

MemoryDB supports Redis/Valkey-style ACLs to limit command access per user.

```
aws memorydb create-user \
  --user-name ml-app \
  --access-string "on ~ml:* +get +set
+ft.search +ft.aggregate" \
  --authentication-mode Type=password
Passwords=myStrongPass123
```

Then attach user to an ACL:

```
aws memorydb create-acl \
  --acl-name ml-acl \
  --user-names ml-app
```

261

- **In-transit**: Always enable TLS (default).

- **At-rest**: MemoryDB encrypts data using AWS KMS.

To use a customer-managed KMS key:

```
aws memorydb create-cluster \
  --cluster-name secure-cluster \
  --kms-key-id arn:aws:kms:us-east-1:123456789012:key/abcde-1234
```

High Availability and Multi-AZ

MemoryDB is **natively Multi-AZ** when replicas are used. For each shard, at least one replica should be in a different AZ.

Setting	Best Practice
Shards	≥ 2
Replicas per shard	≥ 1
AZs in subnet group	≥ 2
TLS	Enabled
Snapshots	Scheduled daily for DR

Use the following for automatic snapshots:

```
aws memorydb update-cluster \
  --cluster-name ml-prod-cluster \
  --snapshot-retention-limit 7 \
  --snapshot-window "04:00-05:00"
```

Monitoring and Troubleshooting

Use **Amazon CloudWatch** and **CloudTrail** for observability.

Key Metrics to Watch

Metric	Description
DatabaseMemoryUsagePercentage	Memory pressure
CurrConnections	Application concurrency
EngineCPUUtilization	CPU health
Evictions	Signs of memory shortage
ReplicationLag	Data sync issues between replicas

Logging

Enable API logging with CloudTrail:

```
aws cloudtrail create-trail \
  --name memorydb-trail \
  --s3-bucket-name my-memorydb-logs
```

263

Secure VPC Access

MemoryDB runs in your **Amazon VPC**, ensuring network isolation.

Network Configuration

- Use **private subnets**

- Restrict access via **security groups**

- Optionally use **AWS PrivateLink** (VPC endpoints)

Example: EC2 Access from Same VPC

```
# EC2 security group
Inbound Rule: TCP port 6379 from MemoryDB
security group
```

Tagging and Cost Tracking

Use tags to organize clusters and associate them with teams, environments, or ML use cases.

```
aws memorydb tag-resource \
  --resource-arn arn:aws:memorydb:us-east-
1:111111111111:cluster/ml-prod-cluster \
  --tags Key=env,Value=production
Key=team,Value=ml
Key=usecase,Value=vectorsearch
```

264

Use tags with **AWS Cost Explorer** or **budgets** for chargeback.

Cluster Topologies for ML Architectures

Topology	Use Case	Description
Single shard, single replica	Dev/Test	Lightweight cluster
Multi-shard, Multi-AZ	Production RAG or Feature Store	High availability and scalability
Multi-region (future)	Cross-continent AI apps	For global low-latency inference

Summary

When used correctly, Amazon MemoryDB can become a core real-time data layer in your ML architecture. To get the most from it:

- **Design for scaling** using shards and replicas

- **Secure your cluster** with ACLs, VPC, and IAM

- **Monitor resource usage** and automate backups

- **Use tagging** for cost transparency and governance

With these patterns, MemoryDB becomes a secure, high-performance memory layer for powering intelligent applications at scale.

Chapter 27: Machine Learning Templates and Connectors (SageMaker, Bedrock)

Amazon OpenSearch Service (AOS) plays an increasingly pivotal role in machine learning (ML) workflows—not just as a search and analytics engine, but as a powerful vector-aware data plane integrated with AWS ML services. In this chapter, we explore how OpenSearch Service integrates with **Amazon SageMaker** and **Amazon Bedrock** using **ML templates and connectors** to enable AI-powered search, inference, and data enrichment pipelines.

We'll cover the architecture, configuration, and deployment of ML connectors in OpenSearch, along with real-world examples and best practices for intelligent data workflows.

Contents:

- ML in OpenSearch: Concepts and Architecture

- Overview of ML Connectors

- Using ML Templates with SageMaker

- Using ML Templates with Bedrock

- Sample Deployment: Semantic Search with SageMaker Endpoint

- Best Practices for Model Integration

- Monitoring and Scaling Inference Pipelines

ML in OpenSearch: Concepts and Architecture

OpenSearch ML is powered by the **ML Commons** plugin, which enables tasks like:

- Model training and deployment

- Inference execution

- Semantic and vector-based search

- Anomaly detection and forecasting

A core part of this capability is **external ML connector support**, which enables you to **call SageMaker or Bedrock models** directly from OpenSearch pipelines or index processors.

Diagram: ML Connector Integration

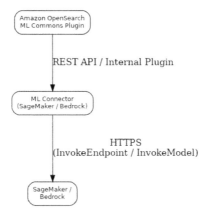

Overview of ML Connectors

OpenSearch ML connectors are lightweight configurations that define:

- The model provider (SageMaker or Bedrock)

- Model ID or endpoint

- Payload format (JSON, Base64, etc.)

- Authentication details (IAM roles or credentials)

Once configured, you can call these connectors directly via the OpenSearch REST API or integrate them into ingestion pipelines.

Supported Connectors

Provider	Supported Models	Use Cases

269

| SageMaker | Any deployed endpoint (custom or JumpStart) | Inference, NLP, image processing |
| Bedrock | Claude, Titan, Llama, Mistral, etc. | Generative AI, LLMs, embeddings |

Using ML Templates with SageMaker

SageMaker integration is ideal for advanced users who train or fine-tune their own models.

Step 1: Create a SageMaker Model Endpoint

You can deploy a model using a SageMaker notebook, SDK, or the console:

```
import sagemaker
from sagemaker.model import Model

model = Model(
    image_uri='763104351884.dkr.ecr.us-east-1.amazonaws.com/pytorch-inference:1.10.0-cpu-py38',
    model_data='s3://my-bucket/my-model.tar.gz',

role='arn:aws:iam::123456789012:role/SageMakerExecutionRole'
)
```

```
predictor =
model.deploy(instance_type='ml.m5.large',
endpoint_name='my-bert-endpoint')
```

Step 2: Define an ML Connector in OpenSearch

```
PUT _plugins/_ml/connectors
{
  "name": "sagemaker-bert",
  "description": "Connector for BERT model
hosted on SageMaker",
  "version": 1,
  "protocol": "aws_sigv4",
  "parameters": {
    "region": "us-east-1",
    "service": "sagemaker",
    "endpoint":
"https://runtime.sagemaker.us-east-
1.amazonaws.com/endpoints/my-bert-
endpoint/invocations"
  }
}
```

Using ML Templates with Bedrock

Amazon Bedrock makes it easy to integrate **foundation models (FMs)** like Claude, Titan, or Mistral with OpenSearch.

Step 1: Set Up Access to Bedrock

Ensure the IAM role used by OpenSearch has the `bedrock:InvokeModel` permission.

Step 2: Create an ML Connector for Bedrock

```
PUT _plugins/_ml/connectors
{
  "name": "bedrock-claude",
  "protocol": "aws_sigv4",
  "parameters": {
    "region": "us-east-1",
    "service": "bedrock",
    "endpoint": "https://bedrock-
runtime.us-east-
1.amazonaws.com/model/anthropic.claude-
v2/invoke"
  }
}
```

Step 3: Run Inference Using the Connector

```
POST _plugins/_ml/_predict
{
  "connector_id": "bedrock-claude",
  "input": {
    "prompt": "Summarize the following
customer review...",
    "max_tokens": 200
```

```
    }
}
```

This enables **text summarization**, **question answering**, or **document embedding** as part of a search pipeline.

Sample Deployment: Semantic Search with SageMaker

Here's how to implement semantic search using a SageMaker-hosted embedding model and vector search in OpenSearch.

1. Create a SageMaker endpoint (e.g., sentence-transformers model).

2. Create an OpenSearch ML connector for the endpoint.

3. Ingest documents with vector embeddings:

```
from sentence_transformers import
SentenceTransformer
import boto3

model = SentenceTransformer('all-MiniLM-L6-v2')
texts = ["OpenSearch is a great search engine",
"Amazon SageMaker handles ML at scale"]

vectors = model.encode(texts)

# Index into OpenSearch
```

```
for i, text in enumerate(texts):
    doc = {
        "text": text,
        "text_vector": vectors[i].tolist()
    }

requests.put(f"https://{OPENSEARCH_ENDPOINT}/my
-index/_doc/{i+1}", json=doc)
```

4. Configure your index with k-NN settings:

```
PUT my-index
{
  "settings": {
    "index": {
      "knn": true
    }
  },
  "mappings": {
    "properties": {
      "text_vector": {
        "type": "knn_vector",
        "dimension": 384
      }
    }
  }
}
```

5. Run vector search queries using the knn API:

```
POST my-index/_search
{
  "size": 3,
  "query": {
    "knn": {
      "text_vector": {
        "vector": [0.123, 0.456, ...],
        "k": 3
      }
    }
  }
}
```

Best Practices for Model Integration

- **Use IAM roles** instead of static credentials for secure access.

- **Cache embeddings** where possible to avoid redundant inference costs.

- For real-time workloads, **monitor latency** on the SageMaker or Bedrock side.

- **Scale endpoints horizontally** in SageMaker if throughput is high.

- Use **Auto-Tune** on OpenSearch domains to optimize memory and thread pools for ML traffic.

Monitoring and Scaling Inference Pipelines

OpenSearch ML usage can be monitored using:

- **CloudWatch metrics** (model invocation time, connector errors)

- **OpenSearch ML stats API**
  (`_plugins/_ml/_stats`)

- **Custom dashboards** in OpenSearch Dashboards

To scale:

- Use **multiple endpoints** with weighted routing.

- Use **Lambda or Step Functions** to orchestrate large inference batches.

- Combine with **OpenSearch ingestion pipelines** for real-time processing.

Summary

By integrating OpenSearch Service with SageMaker and Bedrock using ML templates and connectors, you can operationalize ML models at scale—enabling everything from semantic search to generative summarization. These capabilities make OpenSearch a powerful component in intelligent data architectures on AWS.

Chapter 28: Vector and Semantic Search at Scale

As machine learning and AI applications mature, **vector and semantic search** capabilities are becoming indispensable in data-driven systems. These techniques enable searching not just by keywords, but by **meaning** and **context**, unlocking powerful new experiences in applications like recommendation engines, anomaly detection, and intelligent document retrieval.

Amazon OpenSearch Service (AOS) provides native support for vector search through its **k-NN plugin** and integrates seamlessly with **ML embeddings**, allowing you to build **scalable semantic search architectures** on fully managed infrastructure.

In this chapter, we'll explore the building blocks, architecture, and best practices for deploying vector and semantic search at scale using OpenSearch.

Contents

- Real-World Use Case: Intelligent Document Search

- Best Practices and Monitoring

Understanding Vector Search and Embeddings

In semantic search, text is first transformed into numerical representations (vectors) using machine learning models like BERT, GPT, or Sentence Transformers. These **embeddings** capture the meaning of the input and can be compared using vector similarity algorithms.

For example:

Text	Embedding (vector)
"How to reset my password?"	`[0.12, -0.33, 0.91, ...]`
"Change login credentials"	`[0.11, -0.32, 0.88, ...]`

Both embeddings are close in vector space—indicating similar meaning.

OpenSearch supports storing and searching such vectors using the **k-Nearest Neighbors (k-NN)** plugin.

OpenSearch k-NN Engine Overview

OpenSearch's k-NN plugin leverages two highly efficient engines for similarity search:

279

- **Faiss (Facebook AI Similarity Search)**: Ideal for dense vector search.

- **nmslib (Non-Metric Space Library)**: Better for sparse or high-dimensional vectors.

Vector Search Configurations

- **k-NN indexes**: Specialized index types that store vectors.

- **knn_vector field type**: Holds the dense vector representation.

- **ANN (Approximate Nearest Neighbor)** algorithms like HNSW for performance.

Creating k-NN Indexes and Storing Vectors

Let's walk through creating a semantic search index.

Step 1: Create a k-NN Enabled Index

```
PUT /support-articles
{
  "settings": {
    "index": {
      "knn": true,
      "knn.algo_param.ef_search": 100,
```

```
      "knn.algo_param.ef_construction":
256
    }
  },
  "mappings": {
    "properties": {
      "title": { "type": "text" },
      "content": { "type": "text" },
      "embedding": {
        "type": "knn_vector",
        "dimension": 384
      }
    }
  }
}
```

⚙ Use 384 if using `all-MiniLM-L6-v2`
from `sentence-transformers`.

Step 2: Generate Embeddings

Use Amazon SageMaker or a local model:

```
from sentence_transformers import
SentenceTransformer
model = SentenceTransformer("all-MiniLM-
L6-v2")
vec = model.encode("How do I change my
password?")
```

Step 3: Index Documents with Vectors

```
PUT /support-articles/_doc/1
{
  "title": "Resetting your password",
  "content": "To reset your password, go
to settings...",
  "embedding": [0.12, -0.33, 0.91, ...]
}
```

Performing Vector and Hybrid Searches

Vector Search with k-NN

```
POST /support-articles/_search
{
  "size": 3,
  "query": {
    "knn": {
      "embedding": {
        "vector": [0.12, -0.33, 0.91,
...],
        "k": 3
      }
    }
  }
}
```

Hybrid Search (Vector + Keyword)

```
POST /support-articles/_search
{
  "size": 5,
  "query": {
    "bool": {
      "must": [
        {
          "match": {
            "content": "account"
          }
        },
        {
          "knn": {
            "embedding": {
              "vector": [0.12, -0.33,
0.91, ...],
              "k": 3
            }
          }
        }
      ]
    }
  }
}
```

This hybrid approach combines **semantic relevance** and **keyword precision**, improving search quality.

Architecting for Scalability and Performance

To scale vector search:

1. Choose Optimized Instances

Use **OpenSearch-optimized instances (e.g., r7g, m6g)** with high memory and compute.

2. Use HNSW for Large Scale

Set algorithm parameters in index settings:

```
"index": {
  "knn": true,
  "knn.algo_param.ef_search": 512,
  "knn.algo_param.m": 32
}
```

3. Tune Sharding Strategy

Split vector-heavy workloads across multiple shards and nodes. Use `index.routing.allocation.total_shards_per_node` to prevent imbalance.

4. Storage Tiering

Use **UltraWarm** or **cold storage** for archival text data while keeping vector indexes in hot storage.

5. Monitor Query Load

Use **CloudWatch** metrics like `SearchLatency`, `KNNQueryCount`, and `JVMHeapPressure` to detect scaling bottlenecks.

Real-World Use Case: Intelligent Document Search

Scenario: A customer support platform wants to auto-suggest the most relevant KB articles based on user queries.

Architecture

User Query

Embed Text
(SageMaker / Bedrock)

Search via k-NN API

OpenSearch Domain
- Vector Index
- Text Metadata

Return Top Matches

Key Elements:

- Text embeddings generated on-the-fly

- Indexed articles pre-embedded and stored in OpenSearch

- Frontend presents ranked suggestions

Best Practices and Monitoring

☑ **Use float32 encoding** for high-precision embeddings
☑ **Batch embeddings** to reduce API calls
☑ **Use appropriate dimension sizes** (128–1024)
☑ **Retain original text fields** for explainability
☑ **Enable slow logs** for vector queries (`knn_query`)
☑ **Use reserved instance pricing** for cost efficiency

CloudWatch Metrics to Monitor:

- `KNNQueryCount`

- `SearchLatency`

- `CPUUtilization`

- `JVMHeapPressure`

- `SegmentCount`

Summary

OpenSearch Service empowers you to build scalable, production-grade **vector and semantic search** solutions using native k-NN indexing and ML model integrations. From document search to recommendation engines and chat-based UIs, vector search is the foundation for intelligent data workflows in modern applications.

Chapter 29: Learning to Rank and Natural Language Queries

As AI-powered search becomes mainstream, optimizing search result relevance using **Learning to Rank (LTR)** and enabling intuitive **natural language querying** are crucial for modern applications. Amazon OpenSearch Service (AOS) provides built-in capabilities for both—combining scalable search infrastructure with machine learning and natural language interfaces.

This chapter focuses on how to implement, train, deploy, and monitor LTR models within OpenSearch, and how to enable **natural language search** using **semantic embeddings**, **LLMs**, and **query understanding techniques**.

Contents

- Overview of Learning to Rank in OpenSearch

- LTR Workflow: Feature Extraction to Re-Ranking

- Training and Uploading LTR Models

- Querying with LTR-Enhanced Search

- Natural Language Query Interfaces

- Integrating with LLMs (SageMaker / Bedrock)

- Best Practices and Optimization

Overview of Learning to Rank in OpenSearch

Learning to Rank is a machine learning technique used to reorder search results based on relevance predictions. OpenSearch supports LTR through the **ML Commons plugin**, allowing you to:

- Train ranking models (e.g., XGBoost, LightGBM)

- Upload and register models

- Associate models with queries

- Re-rank the top K documents based on features

Use cases include:

- Personalized search

- E-commerce product ranking

- Customer support article relevance

LTR Workflow: From Features to Ranking

OpenSearch's LTR pipeline involves the following steps:

1. **Feature Extraction**: Define how to extract query-document features (e.g., BM25 score, document

popularity).

2. **Model Training**: Train an LTR model externally using tools like XGBoost or LightGBM.

3. **Model Upload**: Register the model in OpenSearch.

4. **Feature Log Generation**: Generate logs of features and relevance labels for retraining.

5. **Search with Re-ranking**: Use LTR re-ranker to reorder the top N documents.

Architecture

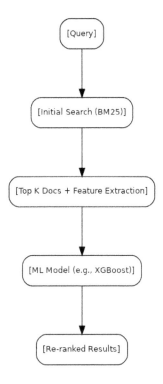

Training and Uploading LTR Models

Step 1: Feature Extraction Example

```
PUT _ltr/_featureset/article_features
{
  "featureset": {
    "features": [
      {
        "name": "bm25_score",
        "params": ["keywords"],
        "template_language": "mustache",
        "template": {
```

```
          "match": {
            "content": "{{keywords}}"
          }
        }
      },
      {
        "name": "doc_views",
        "params": ["doc_id"],
        "template_language": "mustache",
        "template": {
          "term": {
            "doc_id": "{{doc_id}}"
          }
        }
      }
    ]
  }
}
```

Step 2: Train Model Externally (XGBoost Example)

```
import xgboost as xgb

dtrain = xgb.DMatrix(X_train, label=y_train)
params = {'objective': 'rank:pairwise', 'eta': 0.1,
'gamma': 1.0, 'min_child_weight': 0.1}
model = xgb.train(params, dtrain,
num_boost_round=100)

model.save_model('ltr-model.json')
```

Step 3: Upload Model to OpenSearch

```
curl -X POST
"https://DOMAIN/_plugins/_ml/models/_register" -H
'Content-Type: application/json' -d '
{
  "name": "article-ltr-model",
  "model_format": "xgboost_json",
  "model_content_base64": "BASE64_ENCODED_MODEL"
}'
```

Querying with LTR-Enhanced Search

Once a model is associated with a feature set, apply it to
re-rank search results.

```
POST /support-articles/_search
{
  "query": {
    "bool": {
      "must": [
        { "match": { "content": "forgot
password" } }
      ]
    }
  },
  "rescore": {
    "window_size": 50,
    "query": {
      "rescore_query": {
        "ltr": {
          "model": "article-ltr-model",
```

```
      "params": {
        "keywords": "forgot password"
      }
    }
  },
  "query_weight": 0.3,
  "rescore_query_weight": 1.5
  }
 }
}
```

This reorders the top 50 results using the LTR model while still leveraging BM25 scoring.

Natural Language Query Interfaces

Natural language querying goes beyond keywords—supporting conversational phrases like:

- "How can I reset my login credentials?"

- "Show me recent updates to tax policy."

To enable this, OpenSearch can:

- **Embed queries using ML models**

- **Use transformers or LLMs to rewrite or summarize queries**

- **Map natural language to structured filters or DSL queries**

Architecture: NLP Query Flow

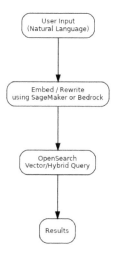

Integrating with LLMs (SageMaker / Bedrock)

Use Amazon Bedrock or SageMaker to enhance natural language querying:

Example: Rewriting Natural Language Query (Claude)

```
POST _plugins/_ml/_predict
{
  "connector_id": "bedrock-claude",
  "input": {
```

```
    "prompt": "Rewrite the following for
search: 'How do I view last month's
invoice?'"
  }
}
```

Output: `"view invoice date: last
month"`

Use this rewritten query as input for structured search in
OpenSearch.

Best Practices and Optimization

LTR Best Practices

- Start with a small feature set, expand iteratively

- Evaluate offline with NDCG/MAP scores

- Use `rescore` window carefully to balance latency vs. accuracy

- Regularly retrain models using fresh logs

Natural Language Querying Tips

- Cache embeddings and rewritten queries

- Combine keyword and vector search (hybrid)

- Use embeddings trained on your domain data

- Monitor query performance and fallback to keyword search when needed

Summary

Combining **Learning to Rank** with **Natural Language Interfaces** unlocks the full potential of search in AI/ML applications. OpenSearch provides robust tools for both— enabling you to optimize relevance and offer conversational, intelligent querying at scale.

Part VI – Cross-Service Architectures and Case Studies

Chapter 30: Anomaly Detection and Real-Time AI with OpenSearch

Modern enterprises require continuous monitoring of systems, applications, and user behavior to detect anomalies and take action in real time. Amazon OpenSearch Service (AOS) delivers built-in **Anomaly Detection (AD)** and supports **real-time AI inference pipelines**, enabling intelligent, automated responses to outliers and trends in your data.

In this chapter, we'll explore how to use OpenSearch for real-time anomaly detection, integrate with ML models for inference, and build end-to-end pipelines that support intelligent observability and alerting.

Contents

- Introduction to Anomaly Detection in OpenSearch

- Architecture for Real-Time Anomaly Detection

- Creating and Managing Detectors

- Real-Time AI Pipelines with OpenSearch Ingestion

- Streaming AI Workflows with Lambda and SageMaker

- Visualization and Alerting

- Best Practices and Scaling Guidance

Introduction to Anomaly Detection in OpenSearch

OpenSearch's AD capability is powered by the **ML Commons plugin**, using an unsupervised Random Cut Forest (RCF) algorithm to identify outliers based on historical patterns.

Use cases include:

- CPU/memory/disk anomalies in infrastructure metrics

- Sudden drops or spikes in sales, transactions, or traffic

- Fraud or intrusion detection in security logs

- Sensor drift in IoT applications

Key Features:

- Time series support

- Single- and multi-entity detectors

- Real-time streaming evaluation

- Integration with OpenSearch Dashboards

- Alerting and visualization built-in

Architecture for Real-Time Anomaly Detection

The following architecture outlines how AD integrates with ingestion pipelines and alerting engines:

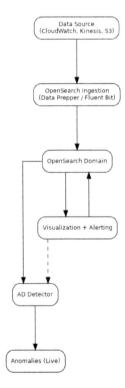

OpenSearch can continuously evaluate data streams and flag anomalies via detectors that work across indices, dimensions, or time windows.

Creating and Managing Detectors

Step 1: Enable ML Commons

Ensure your domain has ML Commons enabled.

```
PUT _cluster/settings
{
  "persistent": {

"plugins.ml_commons.only_run_on_ml_node":
false
  }
}
```

Step 2: Define a Detector

You can use the REST API or OpenSearch Dashboards:

```
POST
_plugins/_anomaly_detection/_detectors
{
  "name": "cpu-usage-detector",
```

```
  "description": "Detect CPU usage
anomalies",
  "time_field": "timestamp",
  "indices": ["infra-metrics"],
  "feature_attributes": [
    {
      "feature_name": "avg_cpu",
      "feature_enabled": true,
      "aggregation_query": {
        "avg_cpu": {
          "avg": {
            "field": "cpu_percent"
          }
        }
      }
    }
  ],
  "detection_interval": {
    "period": {
      "interval": 1,
      "unit": "Minutes"
    }
  },
  "window_delay": {
    "period": {
      "interval": 1,
      "unit": "Minutes"
    }
  }
}
```

Step 3: Start the Detector

```
POST
_plugins/_anomaly_detection/detectors/<det
ector-id>/_start
```

Detectors will continuously evaluate new data and flag outliers in near real time.

Real-Time AI Pipelines with OpenSearch Ingestion

Using **OpenSearch Ingestion** (OSI), you can enrich incoming data with ML inference, filtering, and transformation before indexing.

Example: Ingest Logs and Detect Security Threats

```
pipeline:
  name: security-anomaly-pipeline
  source:
    s3:
      bucket: "my-log-bucket"
  processor:
    - grok: { match: { "message":
"%{IP:ip} - %{GREEDYDATA:log}" } }
    - ml-inference:
```

```
       connector: "sagemaker-threat-
detector"
       input_field: "log"
       output_field: "threat_score"
  sink:
    opensearch:
      index: "security-logs"
```

This pipeline:

- Extracts structured fields from logs

- Uses a SageMaker model to assign a threat score

- Stores results in an OpenSearch index for further AD and alerting

---

Streaming AI Workflows with Lambda and SageMaker

For custom real-time ML, you can integrate OpenSearch with **Amazon Kinesis + AWS Lambda + SageMaker**:

Architecture

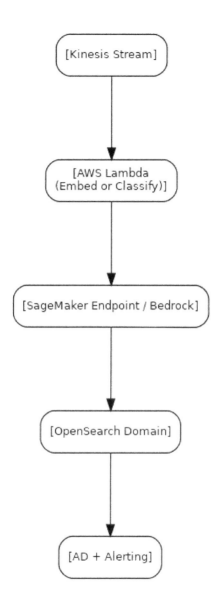

Lambda Example: Classify Transaction Risk

```python
import boto3
import json
import requests

def lambda_handler(event, context):
    for record in event['Records']:
        data =
json.loads(record['kinesis']['data'])
        payload = {"inputs":
data['message']}

        response = requests.post(

'https://<OpenSearchEndpoint>/transactions
/_doc/',
            auth=('admin', 'password'),
            json=payload
        )

    return {'statusCode': 200}
```

This setup lets you use real-time classification and anomaly detection for financial, e-commerce, or IoT pipelines.

Visualization and Alerting

View Detectors and Results

Use **OpenSearch Dashboards > Anomaly Detection**:

- Monitor detectors in real time

- Plot anomaly scores and confidence intervals

- Filter and correlate by dimension (e.g., host, region)

Enable Alerts

Use **Alerting plugin** with custom triggers:

```
{
  "trigger": {
    "query": {
      "match": { "anomaly_grade": { "gte":
0.7 } }
    }
  },
  "actions": [
    {
      "name": "Notify Security Team",
      "destination_id": "slack-channel",
      "message_template": {
        "source": "High anomaly detected
in server logs!"
      }
    }
  ]
```

```
}
```

You can send alerts via SNS, Slack, PagerDuty, or Lambda for automated remediation.

Best Practices and Scaling Guidance

Area	Recommendation
Shards	Use 1–2 shards per 10GB of data for AD
Memory	Monitor JVM pressure if detectors run frequently
Features	Limit to 5–10 features per detector
Entities	Use category fields like host, region for multi-entity
Storage	Archive raw logs in UltraWarm/Cold for historical trends
Security	Use fine-grained access control on indices with detectors
Evaluation	Use anomaly grade + confidence to filter false positives

---

Summary

Amazon OpenSearch Service delivers robust, real-time anomaly detection and AI integration capabilities for observability, security, and operational intelligence. By combining ingestion pipelines, SageMaker/Bedrock models, and real-time detectors, you can build AI-native data flows with automated insights and responses.

In the next chapter, we'll cover **Security and Governance for AI Workflows in OpenSearch**, diving into access control, encryption, compliance, and operational audit logging.

Chapter 31: End-to-End ML Architecture: From Ingestion to Inference

Designing a successful AI/ML solution on AWS requires more than just choosing the right model or tuning hyperparameters—it demands a **robust, scalable, and secure data pipeline** that moves data from ingestion through feature engineering, training, inference, and continuous monitoring. In this chapter, we'll explore how to architect an end-to-end machine learning pipeline using AWS-managed database services as the backbone for data operations.

You'll learn how to combine services like **Aurora, DocumentDB, Neptune, MemoryDB, and OpenSearch** with SageMaker, Lambda, and S3 to create a full ML workflow that's modular, performant, and production-ready.

Overview of the End-to-End Pipeline

An end-to-end ML architecture typically includes the following stages:

1. **Data Ingestion**

2. **Data Storage & Processing**

3. **Feature Engineering**

4. **Model Training**

5. **Model Deployment**

6. **Inference & Serving**

7. **Monitoring & Feedback Loop**

Let's walk through each stage and see how AWS database services plug into the workflow.

Data Ingestion

Data can enter your ML pipeline from multiple sources:

- **Transactional systems (Aurora)**: Capture changes via Activity Streams or log-based exports

- **Event-based sources (DocumentDB Change Streams)**: Detect inserts/updates in real-time

- **Sensor or IoT data (Kinesis, IoT Core)**: Push data into S3 or DynamoDB

- **Web and API logs**: Use Firehose or Lambda to ingest into S3 or OpenSearch

Ingested data is typically staged in **Amazon S3** for durable, scalable storage or streamed directly into operational databases for immediate use.

Data Storage & Processing

Each database serves a different role:

- **Aurora**: Core structured data (orders, transactions, user records)

- **DocumentDB**: User metadata, session data, product catalogs (JSON)

- **Neptune**: Graph data, relationships, influence modeling

- **OpenSearch**: Logs, search queries, clickstream data

- **MemoryDB**: Real-time cache for vector embeddings or session tokens

Data transformations are often handled with **AWS Glue**, **Lambda**, or **Step Functions**, prepping data for feature engineering.

Feature Engineering

This step involves creating useful inputs for your ML models:

- **SQL Queries on Aurora**: Derive aggregates, joins, and time-windowed features

- **Aggregation Pipelines in DocumentDB**: Extract user-level or session features

- **Graph Metrics in Neptune**: Use PageRank, centrality, or community detection

- **Precomputed Embeddings**: Store in MemoryDB or OpenSearch for fast access

- **Custom ETL**: Built using Glue or EMR for large-scale transformation jobs

Processed features are written to **Amazon S3** or a **Feature Store** for training.

Model Training

Training jobs run on **Amazon SageMaker**, optionally using:

- **Input from S3**

- **Glue crawlers to catalog data**

- **Redshift + Zero-ETL Aurora integration** for real-time analytical training

You can also schedule retraining pipelines using **Step Functions** or **Airflow on MWAA** (Managed Workflows for Apache Airflow).

Model Deployment

Once trained, models are deployed to:

- **SageMaker Endpoints** for online inference

- **Lambda Functions** for serverless scoring

- **Batch Transform Jobs** for asynchronous inference

- **OpenSearch / MemoryDB** for embedded models in search pipelines

Deployment includes setting IAM roles, auto-scaling, and defining input/output schemas.

Inference & Serving

Databases come back into play during inference:

- Query recent data from **Aurora or DocumentDB** to pass into the model

- Retrieve embeddings from **MemoryDB** or **OpenSearch**

- Use Lambda to orchestrate inputs, call models, and store predictions

For real-time inference:

```
User request → Lambda → Query DB + Embed →
Call SageMaker → Return Prediction
```

For batch scoring:

```
Daily ETL → Join data → Predict → Store
results in Aurora, DocumentDB, or S3
```

Monitoring & Feedback Loop

Monitoring is essential for model performance and drift detection:

- Use **CloudWatch** to track latency, throughput, and model errors

- Use **Neptune** or **OpenSearch** to analyze behavior graph or prediction trends

- Store feedback (clicks, corrections) in **DocumentDB** or **Aurora** for retraining

- Use **SageMaker Model Monitor** to capture data drift, prediction skew, and bias

This loop closes the lifecycle, enabling continuous improvement through MLOps practices.

Architecture Example: Product Recommendation Engine

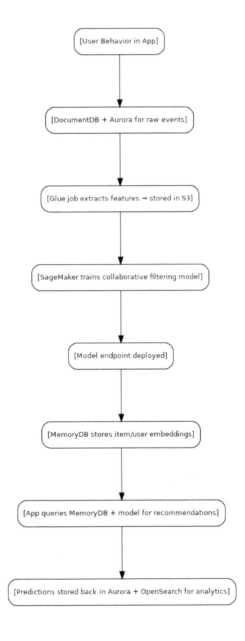

[User Behavior in App]

[DocumentDB + Aurora for raw events]

[Glue job extracts features → stored in S3]

[SageMaker trains collaborative filtering model]

[Model endpoint deployed]

[MemoryDB stores item/user embeddings]

[App queries MemoryDB + model for recommendations]

[Predictions stored back in Aurora + OpenSearch for analytics]

Security and Cost Considerations

- Use **IAM Roles for Service Access**

- **Encrypt data at rest and in transit**

- Apply **VPC isolation** for sensitive workloads

- Use **Serverless** options like Aurora v2, Lambda, and MemoryDB for cost-efficient scaling

Conclusion

An end-to-end ML pipeline is a blend of well-orchestrated components. AWS provides the tools—but the magic lies in assembling them thoughtfully. Whether you're running real-time inference on streaming events or periodically training massive models from historical data, using AWS databases as the backbone ensures your pipeline is both flexible and scalable.

Chapter 32: Real-World Use Cases: Fraud Detection, Recommender Systems, NLP

The power of AWS-managed databases is best seen in action. This chapter explores three high-impact AI/ML applications—**fraud detection**, **recommendation systems**, and **natural language processing (NLP)**—and shows how to design scalable, production-grade solutions using services like **Aurora**, **DocumentDB**, **Neptune**, **MemoryDB**, and **OpenSearch**.

Each use case illustrates architecture patterns, database choices, and integration points with AWS AI/ML services like **SageMaker**, **Bedrock**, and **Lambda**.

Use Case 1: Fraud Detection

Business Need: Detect suspicious transactions or behavioral anomalies in real-time to prevent financial loss or abuse.

Key Challenges:

- Identify subtle patterns across users and devices

- React in milliseconds to suspicious activity

- Learn from historical fraud trends

Recommended AWS Services:

- **Aurora**: Core transactional data

- **Neptune**: Relationship modeling (fraud rings, device reuse)

- **SageMaker**: Real-time ML inference

- **OpenSearch**: Anomaly detection and visual dashboards

Architecture:

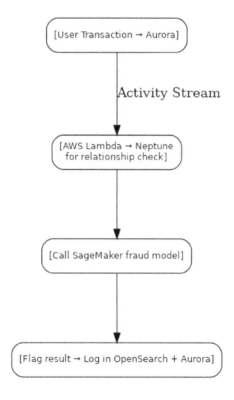

Highlights:

- Use **graph-based features** (e.g., shared IPs, shared devices) via Neptune

- Stream real-time transactions from **Aurora** via Activity Streams

- Trigger ML inference using **Lambda + SageMaker endpoints**

- Surface trends and insights via **OpenSearch dashboards**

Use Case 2: Recommendation Systems

Business Need: Deliver personalized product, content, or media recommendations that adapt to user behavior and preferences.

Key Challenges:

- Mix structured and unstructured user data

- Deliver low-latency recommendations

- Store and retrieve embeddings efficiently

Recommended AWS Services:

- **DocumentDB**: User metadata and interaction logs

- **Neptune**: Relationship mapping and content similarity

- **SageMaker**: Train collaborative filtering or deep learning models

- **MemoryDB / OpenSearch**: Vector search for semantic recommendations

Architecture:

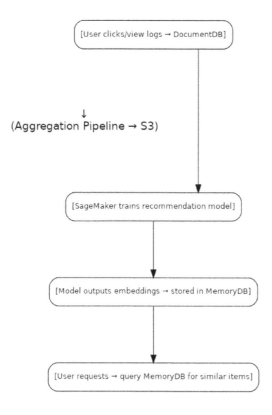

Highlights:

- Store product/user metadata in **DocumentDB**

- Build vector embeddings (e.g., via sentence transformers or matrix factorization)

- Store embeddings in **MemoryDB** for fast lookup using k-NN

- Use **OpenSearch** if you want combined filters + vector ranking

---

Use Case 3: Natural Language Processing (NLP)

Business Need: Extract meaning, intent, and entities from unstructured text for use in chatbots, semantic search, sentiment analysis, and summarization.

Key Challenges:

- Handle large volumes of text

- Use pre-trained or custom LLMs

- Enable search and context-aware retrieval

Recommended AWS Services:

- **OpenSearch**: Full-text + semantic search

- **MemoryDB**: RAG architecture and embedding cache

- **SageMaker / Bedrock**: Foundation model inference

- **DocumentDB**: Store raw and processed documents

Architecture:

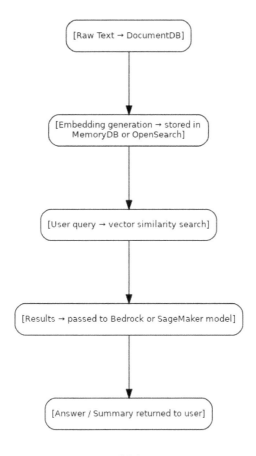

Highlights:

- Use **OpenSearch** for combined full-text and semantic search

- **MemoryDB** accelerates RAG by caching vector results

- **DocumentDB** stores structured and unstructured input

- **Bedrock** offers serverless access to Titan, Claude, or Jurassic-2 models for NLP

Cross-Case Design Patterns

All three use cases share some common architectural building blocks:

Component	Role
Aurora / DocumentDB	Store structured or semi-structured source data
Neptune	Model relationships or user interactions
OpenSearch / MemoryDB	Vector search for embeddings, semantic similarity

SageMaker / Bedrock	Model training and inference
Lambda / Step Functions	Orchestrate workflow and trigger predictions
S3 / Redshift	Data lake for training sets or analytics

Monitoring, Feedback, and Iteration

Each use case benefits from a **continuous feedback loop**:

- Capture predictions, user actions, and errors

- Feed this data back into **Aurora** or **DocumentDB**

- Monitor model drift and retrain in **SageMaker**

- Visualize trends and alerts in **OpenSearch**

By using managed databases and AI services, this loop can be largely automated and scaled to thousands (or millions) of users.

Conclusion

From fraud detection to personalized content to understanding natural language, AWS-managed databases play a crucial role in ML-powered applications.

By combining the right services, architects can build powerful systems that are fast, flexible, and deeply integrated with machine learning workflows.

Chapter 33: Cost Optimization and Performance Tuning for AI Workloads

AI/ML workloads on AWS are powerful, but without careful architectural and operational decisions, they can quickly become expensive and inefficient. Whether you're training large models, running real-time inference, or storing terabytes of features, understanding where your costs originate—and how to tune for performance—is critical.

This chapter focuses on strategies for **cost optimization and performance tuning**, specifically in database-driven AI/ML pipelines. You'll learn how to balance speed, scalability, and budget across services like **Aurora**, **DocumentDB**, **Neptune**, **MemoryDB**, and **OpenSearch**, along with connected tools like **SageMaker**, **Lambda**, and **S3**.

General Cost Optimization Principles for ML Workloads

Regardless of database or model type, these AWS-wide practices apply:

- **Choose serverless or auto-scaling options** where possible (e.g., Aurora Serverless v2, SageMaker Serverless, Lambda)

- **Offload cold data to Amazon S3** and use S3 Select or Athena for ad-hoc access

- **Minimize idle resources** using Step Functions, event triggers, and time-based shutdowns

- **Batch process where real-time isn't needed**, reducing compute hours

- **Use Spot Instances** or Savings Plans for SageMaker training jobs

---

Aurora – Optimizing SQL-Based AI Workloads

Performance Tuning Tips:

- Use **Performance Insights** to identify slow queries and expensive joins

- Use **Cluster Cache Management** for better warm-up times after failover

- Enable **Parallel Query** for complex analytics and feature extraction

- Monitor **Aurora IOPS** and optimize with appropriate instance classes (db.r6g or db.r7g for ML workloads)

Cost Optimization:

- Use **Aurora Serverless v2** for workloads with variable load (e.g., batch inference, feature lookups)

- **Pause-and-resume** dev/test clusters

- Stream data to **Redshift with Zero-ETL** instead of running analytical queries on Aurora

---

DocumentDB – Balancing Flexibility and Cost

Performance Tuning Tips:

- Optimize **indexing strategies** for query-heavy feature extraction

- Avoid frequent large document updates—split into smaller logical entities

- Use **Change Streams** only when needed and throttle consumers

Cost Optimization:

- Right-size your DocumentDB cluster (often overprovisioned by default)

- Offload rarely used data to **S3 or DynamoDB**

- Cache inference results using **MemoryDB** to reduce reads from DocumentDB

Neptune – Tuning Graph-Based Workflows

Performance Tuning Tips:

- Precompute graph features (e.g., PageRank) for batch training

- Use **dedicated read replicas** for analytical queries

- Optimize Gremlin queries: avoid deep traversals or wildcard patterns

Cost Optimization:

- Scale read replicas based on query load

- Archive old nodes/edges not needed for active inference

- Consider alternate storage for low-use graphs (e.g., RDF files in S3 for batch use)

MemoryDB – Real-Time Inference with Budget in Mind

Performance Tuning Tips:

- Use efficient vector dimensions and avoid unnecessary metadata

- Tune query parameters like EF and K for your use case's speed/accuracy tradeoff

- Monitor **memory usage** to prevent out-of-memory crashes

Cost Optimization:

- Use **sharded nodes** to distribute memory cost effectively

- Store only hot embeddings (cold vectors can go to OpenSearch or S3)

- Regularly purge stale or low-value entries

OpenSearch – Smart Search, Smart Budgeting

Performance Tuning Tips:

- Use **index templates** and **mappings** to avoid dynamic field bloat

- Compress source fields (`_source`) if not needed for queries

- Use **k-NN filters** only where necessary; mix with traditional ranking

Cost Optimization:

- Reduce shard count for smaller datasets

- Use **UltraWarm** or **Cold Tier** for logs and historic search data

- Filter data before ingest (via Lambda) to avoid unnecessary writes

---

Inference Cost Strategies

Model inference can become expensive—especially when tied to real-time database queries.

Best Practices:

- Use **batch transforms** for non-time-sensitive scoring

- Cache common inference results in **MemoryDB** or **DynamoDB**

- Use **multi-model endpoints** in SageMaker to consolidate deployments

- Consider **Amazon Bedrock** for shared model access across apps (pay-per-token vs full model hosting)

Training Optimization

Training is often the single largest cost center in AI/ML. You can reduce training time and cost with:

- **Data filtering at the source (Aurora/DocumentDB)** before pushing to S3

- **Feature caching** to avoid recomputation

- **Spot Instances and Managed Spot Training** in SageMaker

- **Hyperparameter tuning jobs with budget constraints**

Also consider techniques like:

- Incremental training

- Transfer learning

- Reuse of pretrained embeddings stored in **OpenSearch** or **MemoryDB**

Monitoring, Autoscaling, and Alerts

Set up:

- **CloudWatch alarms** on CPU, IOPS, memory, and billing

- **Autoscaling policies** for serverless Aurora, Neptune, and SageMaker

- Use **Trusted Advisor** and **Cost Explorer** to track underutilized resources

Also consider **Amazon CloudWatch RUM** or **X-Ray** for tracing and bottleneck analysis in inference paths.

Conclusion

AI/ML systems don't have to be resource hogs—especially when designed with cost-awareness and performance in mind. Each AWS-managed database offers tuning knobs, scaling options, and pricing models tailored to different ML use cases. Mastering these can drastically lower your total cost of ownership while boosting speed, reliability, and developer happiness.

Chapter 34: Security and Compliance Considerations in AI Data Flows

As AI and machine learning systems become deeply embedded in critical business workflows, ensuring **data security** and **regulatory compliance** is no longer optional—it's foundational. AI/ML data flows often involve sensitive personal information, financial records, proprietary models, or real-time behavioral data. When these flows intersect with AWS-managed databases, special care must be taken to enforce end-to-end security across ingestion, storage, training, inference, and retention.

This chapter explores the best practices, AWS tools, and architectural patterns for securing AI/ML pipelines, with a focus on the services discussed throughout this book: **Aurora**, **DocumentDB**, **Neptune**, **MemoryDB**, and **OpenSearch**.

Core Security Principles for AI/ML Pipelines

Security must be applied holistically, across the entire AI lifecycle:

- **Least privilege access**: Grant only the minimum required permissions for each component.

- **Encryption everywhere**: Encrypt data at rest and in transit.

- **Auditability**: Ensure all actions are logged and traceable.

- **Data minimization**: Only process data that's necessary for the ML task.

- **Privacy by design**: Architect with GDPR, HIPAA, or other regulatory compliance in mind.

Identity and Access Management (IAM)

IAM is the backbone of all AWS security. For AI/ML pipelines:

- **SageMaker, Lambda, and Glue** jobs should have tightly scoped IAM roles.

- **Aurora**, **DocumentDB**, and **Neptune** support IAM authentication for client access.

- Use **IAM policies with conditions** (e.g., VPC source IP, time restrictions) for sensitive workloads.

Tip: Use **resource-based policies** for services like OpenSearch or S3 when sharing across accounts.

Encryption Strategies

Every database service used in ML pipelines supports encryption:

Service	Encryption at Rest	Encryption in Transit
Aurora	KMS-managed (default)	SSL/TLS
DocumentDB	KMS-managed (default)	TLS with certs
Neptune	KMS + client TLS	TLS via endpoint config
MemoryDB	KMS-managed	TLS (in-transit encryption required)
OpenSearch	KMS + Node-to-node TLS	HTTPS, fine-grained access

Best Practices:

- Use **customer-managed KMS keys (CMKs)** for higher control

- Rotate encryption keys regularly

- Use **AWS Certificate Manager (ACM)** for TLS certificates in custom domains

---

Secure Ingestion and Processing

337

When ingesting data into your ML pipeline:

- Use **HTTPS** and **VPC endpoints** for secure service access

- Avoid placing ingestion points on the public internet

- Use **API Gateway with Cognito or IAM auth** for ingestion APIs

- For real-time streams (e.g., Aurora Activity Streams, DocumentDB Change Streams), process via **Lambda in a private subnet**

Avoid: Writing raw sensitive logs to unsecured S3 buckets or unencrypted Kinesis streams.

Data Residency and Sovereignty

If your organization operates under strict regulatory requirements (e.g., healthcare, finance, public sector):

- Use **region-specific deployments** of all services

- Avoid cross-region data transfers unless encrypted and audited

- Use **VPC endpoints** and **PrivateLink** to avoid traversing public internet

Use **AWS Organizations** with **Service Control Policies (SCPs)** to enforce compliance guardrails across accounts.

Protecting Model Inputs and Outputs

Model inputs and outputs can be as sensitive as the training data itself:

- **Input data** should be validated and sanitized to avoid poisoning attacks

- **Model responses** should be logged securely, with PII redaction if necessary

- Use **Amazon Macie** to detect and redact sensitive data in stored logs (e.g., from OpenSearch or S3)

- Use **SageMaker Model Monitor** to detect data drift or anomalous behavior that may indicate abuse

MemoryDB or **OpenSearch**, often used in RAG and semantic search, should enforce **query quotas**, **access filters**, and **field-level security**.

Auditing, Monitoring, and Logging

All components in your pipeline should be observable:

- **Enable CloudTrail** for all database access, model invocations, and role assumptions

- Use **CloudWatch Logs and Metrics** to track suspicious spikes or anomalies

- Use **Neptune Audit Logs**, **Aurora audit plugin**, and **DocumentDB event logging**

- Monitor for IAM misconfigurations or over-privileged roles using **AWS Config** and **Access Analyzer**

For regulated environments, export logs to **S3** and archive them with **Object Lock** for immutability.

Compliance Tools and Services

AWS provides a suite of services for automating compliance alignment:

- **AWS Artifact** – Download compliance reports (HIPAA, SOC, PCI, ISO, etc.)

- **Amazon Macie** – Discover and protect PII/PHI in S3

- **AWS Config + Conformance Packs** – Enforce compliance policies automatically

- **Security Hub** – Aggregate and prioritize security alerts

- **Audit Manager** – Automate evidence collection for audits

Integrate these into your CI/CD pipelines for model deployments or database migrations to ensure everything stays compliant from dev to prod.

Isolating Sensitive Workloads

Use **multi-account architecture** with AWS Organizations:

- One account for ingestion and preprocessing

- Another for model training and experimentation

- A separate account for production inference

Enforce **cross-account access via IAM roles** with explicit trust relationships. Use **Service Control Policies (SCPs)** to prevent accidental exposure.

Conclusion

Security and compliance are not afterthoughts—they're design goals from the very first decision in your ML pipeline. With AWS's robust security model, fine-grained access controls, encryption mechanisms, and compliance tooling, you can build AI/ML systems that meet the strictest industry and government standards.

Chapter 35: Future of Databases in Generative AI on AWS

Generative AI is not just a new wave of innovation—it's a paradigm shift. Foundation models, large language models (LLMs), and multimodal systems are redefining how machines understand, generate, and interact with information. In this transformation, **databases are no longer just storage engines**—they're **intelligent, real-time data hubs** that enable context-aware, semantic, and dynamic interactions.

This chapter explores the evolving role of AWS-managed databases in the **future of Generative AI**, highlighting architectural trends, innovations in data systems, and how databases are becoming integral to LLM pipelines, Retrieval-Augmented Generation (RAG), and real-time adaptive systems.

From Static to Semantic: The New Role of Databases

Traditional databases were designed to store facts and respond to precise queries. In generative AI systems, however, databases must:

- Store and retrieve **high-dimensional embeddings**

- Support **semantic similarity**, not just exact match

- Integrate with LLMs for **context retrieval and prompt construction**

343

- Enable **conversational memory** and dynamic personalization

This transition turns databases into active participants in the generation process—fueling LLMs with knowledge, history, and vectorized meaning.

Vector Databases: Core to RAG Architectures

At the heart of many generative AI systems lies **Retrieval-Augmented Generation (RAG)**, where LLMs are grounded with context pulled from databases:

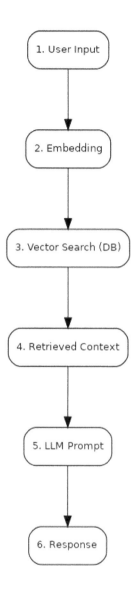

On AWS, vector search is now natively supported across multiple services:

- **Amazon OpenSearch**: k-NN, ANN, semantic ranking

- **Amazon MemoryDB**: Fast, in-memory vector indexing with Redis syntax

- **Amazon DocumentDB**: Vector indexes for JSON-based semantic data

These databases form the retrieval layer for LLM-powered applications—chatbots, search assistants, document Q&A, and more.

Multi-Modal Support: Going Beyond Text

Future LLMs go beyond language—they handle **images, audio, video, and structured data**. Databases must evolve to support:

- **Hybrid indexes**: Text + vector + metadata filters

- **Rich schema support**: For storing and querying multimodal input/output

- **Latency optimization**: For on-demand retrieval across large datasets

For example:

- **OpenSearch** will be used to store image embeddings alongside product catalogs.

- **DocumentDB** might store JSON documents enriched with vector and keyword fields.

- **MemoryDB** could act as a fast-access semantic cache for multimodal dialogue agents.

Real-Time Personalization with Live Data

Generative AI is moving toward **adaptive, real-time personalization**, where LLMs react to live user behavior. This requires:

- **Low-latency database queries** (e.g., MemoryDB, Aurora Serverless)

- **Streaming updates** (Aurora Activity Streams, DocumentDB Change Streams)

- **Short-term memory caching** for session-level interactions

For example, a customer support assistant powered by Bedrock could:

- Pull order history from **Aurora**

- Get recent user clicks from **DocumentDB**

- Match support topics via **vector search in OpenSearch**

- Answer using a Claude model hosted on **Bedrock**

Serverless + Generative AI = Agility at Scale

The move to **serverless infrastructure** aligns perfectly with the bursty, dynamic nature of GenAI applications:

- **Aurora Serverless v2** for sporadic prompt generation or chat memory persistence

- **MemoryDB** for rapid semantic cache spin-ups

- **Lambda + Bedrock** for ephemeral, event-based inference chains

- **OpenSearch Serverless** for scalable vector search APIs

These serverless-native options reduce cost and complexity while enabling scale and responsiveness.

Integration with Bedrock and SageMaker

As AWS continues to consolidate generative AI under **Amazon Bedrock**, we're seeing tight integrations with databases:

- Bedrock plugins accessing **OpenSearch** for contextual grounding

- Chat memory persistence in **Aurora Serverless**

- Document retrieval using **vector indexes in MemoryDB**

- Fine-tuning data pipelines pulling from **S3, DocumentDB, or Redshift**

Future workloads will likely unify under **agent-based frameworks**, where agents use memory, tools, and search—all backed by AWS-managed databases.

Composable AI Systems with Data as the Backbone

Generative AI is increasingly **modular**:

- **Databases as memory**

- **LLMs as reasoning engines**

- **Vector search as context providers**

- **APIs as tools**

In this future, your database isn't just storing rows—it's helping **generate meaning**, **build knowledge**, and **guide the next action**.

Expect to see composable stacks like:

This fusion of structured, semi-structured, and vectorized data is the future of AI-native architectures.

Responsible AI and Governance in Databases

As LLMs consume and generate data, databases must also support:

- **Data lineage tracking**

- **Access audits and field-level encryption**

- **Anonymization pipelines**

- **Retention policies tied to ML artifacts**

AWS services like **Macie**, **CloudTrail**, **IAM**, and **Config** will become part of the GenAI data governance fabric.

Expect databases to natively support:

- **PII masking**

- **Prompt history logging**

- **Inference audit trails**

Conclusion: Your Database Is Your AI Strategy

In the era of Generative AI, the way you structure, store, and retrieve data will define the capabilities of your models. AWS-managed databases are evolving into intelligent, context-aware services that power the next generation of applications—from semantic chat to real-time reasoning.

To future-proof your AI stack:

- Design with **vector search and semantic relevance** in mind

- Treat your databases as **AI co-pilots**, not just data stores

- Embrace **serverless, composable, multi-modal** patterns

Your models will change. Your prompts will evolve. But your **data foundation**—designed thoughtfully—will scale with you into the future.

Appendices

🎁 Appendix A: AWS CLI & SDK Commands for ML Workflows

Practical snippets for building and debugging database-driven AI/ML pipelines on AWS

Whether you're automating data exports, invoking ML endpoints, or performing vector search queries, having a set of ready-to-go AWS CLI and Python SDK (boto3) commands can supercharge your workflow. This appendix provides a curated list of practical, real-world commands used in the field—annotated with explanations and edge-case considerations.

All Python code assumes that the AWS SDK for Python (`boto3`) and required packages are already installed and configured with appropriate credentials.

📋 1. Exporting Data from Aurora to S3 (via Snapshot)

Use Case: Prepare historical data from Aurora for training ML models.

⛭ CLI:

```
aws rds export-task start-export-task \
  --export-task-identifier aurora-export-
ml-2025 \
  --source-arn arn:aws:rds:us-east-
1:123456789012:snapshot:aurora-prod-
snapshot \
  --s3-bucket-name ml-training-datalake \
  --iam-role-arn
arn:aws:iam::123456789012:role/AuroraExpor
tToS3 \
  --kms-key-id arn:aws:kms:us-east-
1:123456789012:key/abc123
```

> *Make sure the snapshot is in* `available`
> *state and the IAM role has*
> `rds:StartExportTask` *and S3 write*
> *permissions.*

🔍 2. Invoking a SageMaker Endpoint with Aurora Data

Use Case: Run real-time ML inference (e.g., fraud score) from SQL data.

🐍 boto3:

```
import boto3
import json
```

```python
sm_runtime = boto3.client('sagemaker-
runtime')

response = sm_runtime.invoke_endpoint(
    EndpointName='fraud-detector-
endpoint',
    ContentType='application/json',
    Body=json.dumps({
        "transaction_id": "abc123",
        "amount": 740.00,
        "location": "Paris"
    })
)

prediction =
json.loads(response['Body'].read())
print("Fraud Score:", prediction)
```

Always validate inputs, especially when querying from Aurora or DocumentDB, to prevent data poisoning or bad JSON.

---

3. Processing DocumentDB Change Streams via Lambda

Use Case: Trigger model inference when a new document is inserted.

boto3 (inside Lambda handler):

```python
def lambda_handler(event, context):
    for record in event['Records']:
        doc = record['fullDocument']
        # Trigger SageMaker or custom
model
        print("Processing new document:",
doc)
```

> ⚠ *Change streams must be explicitly enabled on your DocumentDB collection.*

🌐 4. Creating a Vector Index in MemoryDB (RediSearch)

Use Case: Enable semantic retrieval for real-time RAG applications.

CLI (via redis-cli or MemoryDB proxy):

```
FT.CREATE product_index ON HASH PREFIX 1
product:
  SCHEMA
    name TEXT
    category TEXT
    embedding VECTOR HNSW 6 TYPE FLOAT32
DIM 384 DISTANCE_METRIC COSINE
```

355

redis-py (Python):

```python
from redis.commands.search.field import
TextField, VectorField
from redis.commands.search.indexDefinition
import IndexDefinition, IndexType

index_def =
IndexDefinition(prefix=["product:"],
index_type=IndexType.HASH)
fields = [
    TextField("name"),
    TextField("category"),
    VectorField("embedding", "HNSW", {
        "TYPE": "FLOAT32",
        "DIM": 384,
        "DISTANCE_METRIC": "COSINE"
    })
]

redis_client.ft("product_index").create_in
dex(fields, definition=index_def)
```

Embedding dimension must match your model's output (e.g., 384 for MiniLM).

🧬 5. Performing k-NN Search in OpenSearch

Use Case: Retrieve the top-N semantically similar documents.

CLI (via curl or Postman):

```
curl -X POST "https://your-domain/_search"
-H 'Content-Type: application/json' -d '{
  "size": 3,
  "query": {
    "knn": {
      "vector_field": {
        "vector": [0.25, 0.18, ...],
        "k": 3
      }
    }
  }
}'
```

> 🧠 *Vector field must be indexed with* `index.knn = true` *and appropriate engine (Faiss, NMSLIB, etc.).*

🌐 6. Exporting Neptune Graph to S3 for Offline Feature Engineering

Use Case: Dump graph features like PageRank for ML model training.

CLI:

```
aws neptune-export export-graph \
  --source-cluster-id neptune-graph-
cluster-01 \
  --output-location s3://ml-features-
dump/graph-2025/ \
  --format csv \
  --iam-role-arn
arn:aws:iam::123456789012:role/NeptuneExpo
rtToS3
```

> *You can then run your ML feature*
> *transformation pipelines using Glue or*
> *SageMaker Processing Jobs.*

---

7. Running Batch Transform Jobs in SageMaker

Use Case: Score a full dataset exported from Aurora or DocumentDB.

boto3:

```
sagemaker = boto3.client('sagemaker')

response = sagemaker.create_transform_job(
    TransformJobName='batch-fraud-scores',
    ModelName='fraud-model-2025',
    TransformInput={
        'DataSource': {
```

```
        'S3DataSource': {
            'S3DataType': 'S3Prefix',
            'S3Uri': 's3://ml-
inputs/fraud-data.csv'
            }
        },
        'ContentType': 'text/csv'
    },
    TransformOutput={
        'S3OutputPath': 's3://ml-
outputs/scores/'
    },
    TransformResources={
        'InstanceType': 'ml.m5.large',
        'InstanceCount': 1
    }
)
```

📧 *This is perfect for scoring hundreds of thousands of records from a nightly data export.*

🎯 Summary Table

Task	Tool	Integration Target
Aurora snapshot → S3	CLI	S3, KMS
Realtime inference	boto3	SageMaker Endpoint
Change stream to model	Lambda	DocumentDB + SageMaker

Create/search vector index	redis-py	MemoryDB
Semantic search	curl / boto3	OpenSearch
Export Neptune features	CLI	Neptune → S3
Batch inference	boto3	SageMaker Batch Transform

🧠 Appendix B: ML Integration Recipes

Real-world blueprints for connecting AWS databases to ML systems

This appendix offers hands-on integration recipes that show how AWS-managed databases plug into end-to-end AI/ML workflows. Each recipe includes a real-world use case, architecture, explanation, and implementation tips using services such as **SageMaker**, **Lambda**, **Bedrock**, and more.

🔍 Recipe 1: Aurora Activity Stream → Lambda → SageMaker Fraud Model

Use Case:

Real-time fraud detection from financial transactions stored in Aurora.

Architecture:

```
[Aurora (Activity Stream)]
        ↓
[Amazon Kinesis Data Stream]
        ↓
[AWS Lambda]
        ↓
[Amazon SageMaker Endpoint]
        ↓
[Aurora: Update "fraud_score"]
```

1. **Enable Aurora Activity Streams** on your cluster.

    o   Streams all database activity (inserts/updates) securely via Kinesis.

2. **Configure a Lambda trigger** on the Kinesis stream.

3. **Parse transaction details** in Lambda and call the SageMaker fraud detection model.

4. **Update the transaction row** in Aurora with the `fraud_score` or flag.

Real-World Tip:

Include logic in Lambda to **rate-limit or drop duplicate records** to avoid model overuse during high throughput.

🌐 Recipe 2: DocumentDB Change Streams → RAG Architecture

Use Case:

Semantic Q&A bot that answers based on the latest customer support documents stored in DocumentDB.

Architecture:

```
[DocumentDB (Change Stream)]
```

```
         ↓
[AWS Lambda]
         ↓
[Embedding Generator (e.g., SageMaker)]
         ↓
[Amazon MemoryDB / OpenSearch Vector
Index]
         ↓
[Bedrock / LLM - RAG]
```

Step-by-Step Overview:

1. Enable **change streams** on your DocumentDB collection.

2. Create a **Lambda function** to listen for new/updated documents.

3. Extract content → generate embeddings using:

   ○ A SageMaker endpoint with a sentence transformer

   ○ Or a Bedrock Titan model

4. Store the embeddings in **MemoryDB** or **OpenSearch** under a specific vector key.

5. During inference, retrieve top-k similar documents to inject into the **Bedrock prompt**.

363

Real-World Tip:

If you're using OpenSearch, combine **filtering + vector ranking** to ensure the most relevant context.

🍬 Recipe 3: Neptune → Feature Engineering → SageMaker Training

Use Case:

Build graph-based features (e.g., user connectivity, fraud rings) for predictive model training.

Architecture:

```
[Amazon Neptune]
        ↓
[Gremlin Queries / SPARQL]
        ↓
[Feature CSVs (via Glue or script)]
        ↓
[SageMaker Training Job]
```

Step-by-Step Overview:

1. Run Gremlin queries on Neptune to extract:

   o Centrality

   o Shortest path

- Label propagation

- Degree counts

2. Dump the output to **CSV or Parquet**, then push to **S3**.

3. Use this enriched graph data alongside tabular features in **SageMaker training**.

4. Optionally re-compute graph features periodically via Glue jobs.

Real-World Tip:

Use **graph snapshots** to capture the topology during model training and avoid leakage from future graph mutations.

🔍 Recipe 4: OpenSearch Vector Search → Bedrock Prompt Augmentation

Use Case:

Improve LLM response quality with dynamic, semantic document retrieval.

Architecture:
```
[User Query]
    ↓
[Embedding Generation (Bedrock or Local)]
```

```
                    ↓
[OpenSearch Vector Index → Top-k Matches]
                ↓
[Context + Prompt → Bedrock Model]
                 ↓
[Generated Answer]
```

Step-by-Step Overview:

1. Use an embedding model (Titan, MiniLM, or similar) to convert user queries to vectors.

2. Run a **k-NN search** in OpenSearch against your indexed vector field.

3. Extract the top results, format them into a contextual block.

4. Inject this block into your Bedrock prompt using the `system` or `context` field (depending on model).

5. Generate the response using Titan, Claude, or Jurassic.

Real-World Tip:

Use **OpenSearch filters (e.g., doc type, date range)** alongside vector scoring to improve retrieval relevance.

☑ Summary Table

Recipe Title	Primary DB	ML Service Used	Real-Time ?	Key Value
Aurora Activity Stream → Fraud Detection	Aurora	SageMaker Endpoint	☑	Instant fraud scoring from SQL inserts
DocumentDB → RAG Embedding → Bedrock	DocumentDB	Bedrock, SageMaker	☑	Real-time context refresh for LLMs
Neptune → Feature CSVs → Model Training	Neptune	SageMaker Training	✗	Graph-enhanced batch training
OpenSearch Vector Search → Prompt Augmentation	OpenSearch	Bedrock	☑	Semantically aware chatbots / assistants

367

🔬 **Appendix D:** Benchmarking & Tuning Checklist

Optimize your AI/ML data stack with proven performance insights from AWS and real-world enterprise case studies

Whether you're designing for real-time inference or batch model training, performance tuning is key to maximizing throughput, minimizing latency, and keeping your AWS bill under control. This appendix compiles **benchmark-backed tuning strategies** from AWS documentation and case studies (including Netflix, FINRA, Intuit, and others) to guide you in fine-tuning your AI/ML data pipeline architecture.

▦ General Performance Principles

☑ **Right-size instances:** Start with **burstable or serverless** where possible, then scale up.

☑ **Decouple reads and writes:** Use replicas, caches, and indexing to prevent bottlenecks.

☑ **Use async wherever possible:** For inference, offload to queues or batch transforms.

☑ **Avoid full scans:** Filter early and narrow queries using indexed fields.

☑ **Minimize cold starts:** Pre-warm connections and model endpoints.

☑ **Cache intelligently:** Use MemoryDB for hot features, OpenSearch for semantic data.

Aurora (Relational + SQL ML)

Metric	Recommendation
Instance Type	Use db.r6g or db.r7g for ML-heavy loads
Write Scaling	Use **Aurora Global DB** + write forwarding
Query Speed	Enable **Parallel Query** for large joins
Cold Start	Use aurora_ccm_status() to monitor warmup
Monitoring Tool	**Performance Insights** with top SQL queries
Case Study	**Intuit** used Aurora with ML models and auto-scaling for fraud scoring pipelines

DocumentDB (JSON + Vector)

Metric	Recommendation
Index Strategy	Compound indexes on fields + vector where needed
Insert/Update Load	Break large docs into smaller objects
Vector Indexing	Limit to 256–768 dim, prefer batch updates
Change Stream Tuning	Use **batch windowing** to reduce Lambda triggers
Best Practice	Avoid frequent schema mutations
Case Study	**FINRA** uses DocumentDB to monitor 75B+ trades/day, streaming updates to ML detectors

Neptune (Graph Features for ML)

Metric	Recommendation
Instance Type	Use db.r5.4xlarge+ for analytical queries

Query Language	Gremlin for traversal, SPARQL for declarative logic
Query Tuning	Avoid wildcard filters (*), use fixed paths
Parallel Execution	Use read replicas for long analytics queries
Export for ML	Use Neptune-to-S3 CSV dump for graph feature prep
Case Study	**Netflix** used Neptune for entity-relationship modeling in personalization engines

⚡ MemoryDB (Real-Time Embedding Cache)

Metric	Recommendation
Instance Type	Use db.r6g for balance of price/perf
Vector Tuning	Tune K and EF to balance recall vs speed
Data TTL	Set intelligent TTL for embeddings (RAG use cases)
Shard Scaling	Use horizontal sharding for large embedding sets
Latency Expectation	Expect sub-10ms vector search response
Case Study	**Duolingo** (Redis-based arch) uses in-memory semantic search for instant content matching

🔍 OpenSearch (k-NN, Semantic Search)

Metric	Recommendation
Index Size	≤ 100 million vectors per shard for best performance
Search Type	Use **Faiss or NMSLIB** for dense vector queries
Filter + Vector Combo	Filter first, then apply vector k-NN for best relevance
Warmup Strategy	Pre-load frequently accessed vectors on node boot
Cold Tier Storage	Archive old embeddings using UltraWarm/Cold storage
Case Study	**Redfin** uses OpenSearch for real-time similarity matching in property descriptions

370

Model Inference (SageMaker / Bedrock)

Metric	Recommendation
Batch Size	Tune based on model size—larger batches for GPU
Invocation Type	Use **multi-model endpoints** to reduce cold start cost
Latency Target	Real-time ≤ 100ms, async for >1s model latency
Pre/Post-Processing	Offload to Lambda or Step Functions
Bedrock Models	Pay-per-token → optimize prompt length + embedding reuse
Case Study	**Thomson Reuters** uses SageMaker multi-model endpoints for cost-efficient legal inference APIs

Training + Batch Inference

Metric	Recommendation
Training Runtime	Use **Spot Training** with managed stop/resume
Data Location	Always in the same region as training job (S3 locality)
Feature Store Reads	Use caching for repeated reads or joins
Batch Transform Speed	Use `ml.m5.xlarge`+ instances; parallelize S3 input
Throughput Strategy	Divide data into manifest shards
Case Study	**Airbnb** used distributed training and Glue-based preprocessing pipelines to reduce model training from 3 days to 6 hours

Checklist Summary by Service

Component	Tuning Focus	Cost Risk Factor	Actionable Fix
Aurora	Query tuning, parallel reads	Storage + IOPS	Use Performance Insights

371

DocumentDB	Indexing, vector batch size	Burst compute	Use change streams sparingly
Neptune	Gremlin traversal limits	Over-provisioning	Precompute features
MemoryDB	Vector memory/shard size	Data volume	TTL + prune strategy
OpenSearch	Vector filters, index size	High write throughput	Segment by domain
SageMaker	Endpoint reuse, async scoring	Cold starts	Multi-model endpoint

🔐 Appendix E: IAM Policy Snippets

Ready-to-use permissions for AI/ML pipelines across AWS databases and ML services

Securing access to AWS resources in AI/ML workloads involves crafting precise IAM policies that grant only the permissions necessary for each workflow. This appendix provides **ready-to-use IAM policy snippets** for common AI/ML patterns involving Aurora, DocumentDB, OpenSearch, Neptune, MemoryDB, SageMaker, and more.

All policies follow **least-privilege principles**, are inline-policy compatible, and include optional conditions and tags where relevant.

📖 1. Aurora → S3 Export for ML Training

```
{
  "Version": "2012-10-17",
  "Statement": [
    {
      "Sid": "AllowRDSExport",
      "Effect": "Allow",
      "Action": [
        "rds:StartExportTask",
        "rds:DescribeExportTasks",
        "rds:CancelExportTask"
      ],
      "Resource": "*"
```

```
    },
    {
      "Sid": "AllowS3WriteAccess",
      "Effect": "Allow",
      "Action": [
        "s3:PutObject",
        "s3:GetBucketLocation"
      ],
      "Resource": "arn:aws:s3:::your-s3-
bucket-name/*"
    },
    {
      "Sid": "AllowKMSUsage",
      "Effect": "Allow",
      "Action": [
        "kms:Encrypt",
        "kms:Decrypt",
        "kms:GenerateDataKey"
      ],
      "Resource": "arn:aws:kms:your-
region:your-account-id:key/your-key-id"
    }
  ]
}
```

🧠 2. SageMaker Endpoint Invocation (Lambda or App)

```
{
```

```json
"Version": "2012-10-17",
  "Statement": [
    {
      "Effect": "Allow",
      "Action":
"sagemaker:InvokeEndpoint",
      "Resource": "arn:aws:sagemaker:your-
region:your-account:endpoint/fraud-
detector-endpoint"
    }
  ]
}
```

☑ *Use this in Lambda or API Gateway roles calling ML endpoints.*

📄 3. DocumentDB Change Stream Lambda Trigger

```json
{
  "Version": "2012-10-17",
  "Statement": [
    {
      "Sid": "ReadChangeStream",
      "Effect": "Allow",
      "Action": [
        "docdb:ListCollections",
        "docdb:ListDatabases",
        "docdb:Find",
        "docdb:GetChangeStream"
```

```
      ],
      "Resource": "*"
    }
  ]
}
```

> Combine this with a VPC policy and role
> for Lambda running inside a private subnet.

🧲 4. MemoryDB (Vector Search + Semantic Cache)

```
{
  "Version": "2012-10-17",
  "Statement": [
    {
      "Sid": "AllowMemoryDBAccess",
      "Effect": "Allow",
      "Action": [
        "memorydb:Connect",
        "memorydb:DescribeClusters",
        "memorydb:ListTags"
      ],
      "Resource": "arn:aws:memorydb:your-
region:your-account:cluster/your-cluster"
    }
  ]
}
```

⚙ Typically used for SageMaker, Lambda, or containerized services caching embeddings.

🔍 5. OpenSearch Vector Index Access

```
{
  "Version": "2012-10-17",
  "Statement": [
    {
      "Sid": "SearchOnly",
      "Effect": "Allow",
      "Action": [
        "es:ESHttpPost",
        "es:ESHttpGet"
      ],
      "Resource": "arn:aws:es:your-region:your-account:domain/your-opensearch-domain/*"
    }
  ]
}
```

❙ Attach this to services using vector search (e.g., RAG, semantic chatbots). Use condition keys for field-level security where needed.

377

🔗 6. Neptune Export (Feature Extraction for Training)

```
{
  "Version": "2012-10-17",
  "Statement": [
    {
      "Sid": "AllowGraphExport",
      "Effect": "Allow",
      "Action": [
        "neptune-db:connect",
        "neptune-db:ReadDataViaBulkExport"
      ],
      "Resource": "arn:aws:neptune-
db:your-region:your-account:your-db-
cluster"
    },
    {
      "Sid": "S3ExportWrite",
      "Effect": "Allow",
      "Action": [
        "s3:PutObject"
      ],
      "Resource": "arn:aws:s3:::your-
graph-feature-bucket/*"
    }
  ]
}
```

🎯 7. SageMaker Training + Batch Inference

```json
{
  "Version": "2012-10-17",
  "Statement": [
    {
      "Sid": "AllowTrainingJobs",
      "Effect": "Allow",
      "Action": [
        "sagemaker:CreateTrainingJob",
        "sagemaker:CreateTransformJob",
        "sagemaker:DescribeTrainingJob",
        "sagemaker:DescribeTransformJob"
      ],
      "Resource": "*"
    },
    {
      "Sid": "AllowS3InputOutput",
      "Effect": "Allow",
      "Action": [
        "s3:GetObject",
        "s3:PutObject",
        "s3:ListBucket"
      ],
      "Resource": [
        "arn:aws:s3:::your-training-data/*",
        "arn:aws:s3:::your-training-output/*"
      ]
    }
```

```
    ]
}
```

🔁 *Use this in training roles or Step Functions that initiate batch inference jobs.*

✏️ 8. SageMaker → Bedrock (Model Chaining)

```
{
  "Version": "2012-10-17",
  "Statement": [
    {
      "Sid": "InvokeBedrock",
      "Effect": "Allow",
      "Action": [
        "bedrock:InvokeModel",

"bedrock:InvokeModelWithResponseStream"
      ],
      "Resource": "arn:aws:bedrock:your-
region::foundation-model/anthropic.claude-
v2"
    }
  ]
}
```

⚙️ *Required when building pipelines that use Bedrock models for downstream tasks.*

☑ General Tips for IAM Hygiene

☑ Good Practice	Why it Matters
Use **least privilege**	Reduce risk if credentials are leaked or abused
Tag roles and policies	Easier auditing, especially in ML-heavy orgs
Use **AWS Condition Keys**	Lock access by IP, VPC, service principal, time, etc.
Rotate **access keys**	Especially for long-running training/inference agents
Enable **CloudTrail & Access Analyzer**	Detect privilege escalation and policy misconfiguration

🔍 **Appendix F:** Vector Search Cheat Sheet

Quick reference for using semantic and vector similarity search across AWS databases

---

Vector search has become the cornerstone of modern AI/ML systems—especially Retrieval-Augmented Generation (RAG), semantic recommendation engines, and AI-driven chatbots. This cheat sheet provides you with a **syntax-level comparison**, **pros and cons**, and **use case tips** for working with vector search in **Amazon OpenSearch**, **Amazon MemoryDB**, and **Amazon DocumentDB**.

⚒️ 1. OpenSearch (k-NN / ANN Vector Search)

☑ Syntax (k-NN query)

```
{
  "size": 3,
  "query": {
    "knn": {
      "embedding_vector": {
        "vector": [0.1, 0.2, 0.3, ...],
        "k": 3
      }
    }
  }
}
```

🛠️ Setup Highlights:

- Index type: `"index.knn": true`

- Engine: `faiss`, `nmslib`, or `lucene` (depends on plugin)

- Field type: `knn_vector` with `dimension`, `method`, `similarity`

🧠 Best For:

- RAG pipelines with Bedrock or SageMaker

- Semantic search with filtering (category, user type, etc.)

- NLP chatbots and document summarization

👍 Pros:

- Native support for hybrid search (filter + vector)

- Scales well with horizontal OpenSearch clusters

- Pairs easily with full-text and keyword search

👎 Cons:

- Slower than in-memory for high-volume real-time

- No sub-ms latency without dedicated compute tuning

⭐ 2. MemoryDB (Vector Search via Redis + RediSearch)

☑ Syntax (FT.CREATE and FT.SEARCH)

```
FT.CREATE product_idx ON HASH PREFIX 1
"product:" SCHEMA
  name TEXT
  embedding VECTOR HNSW 6 TYPE FLOAT32 DIM
384 DISTANCE_METRIC COSINE

FT.SEARCH product_idx "*=>[KNN 3
@embedding $vector]"
PARAMS 2 vector $your_vector RETURN 3 name
_score
```

🛠 Setup Highlights:

- **Vector type:** FLOAT32, DIM, DISTANCE_METRIC (COSINE, IP, L2)

- Vector index: HNSW (Hierarchical Navigable Small World)

- Low-latency semantic lookup (<10ms)

- RAG use cases with cached embeddings

- Session-level personalization

- In-memory = blazing fast (~sub-ms)

- Easy integration via `redis-py`, LangChain, or vector libraries

- Scalable via clustering + sharding

- Memory-bound = expensive for massive vector corpora

- Lacks hybrid filtering flexibility (unless encoded manually)

📌 3. DocumentDB (Vector Support in JSON Fields)

☑ Syntax (insertion & querying)

Insert vector field:

```
{
  "_id": "doc1",
  "title": "Sample",
  "embedding": [0.1, 0.2, 0.3, ...]
}
```

Querying via vector index (CLI or shell):

```
db.collection.find({
  $vectorSearch: {
    path: "embedding",
    queryVector: [...],
    k: 3,
    numCandidates: 100,
    distanceMetric: "cosine"
  }
})
```

🛠 Setup Highlights:

- MongoDB 5.0+ vector extensions

- Vector index created using `createIndexes()`
  with `"type": "vector"`

Best For:

- Applications already using DocumentDB for metadata or user content

- Lightweight semantic personalization

- Preprocessing or training-time similarity joins

Pros:

- Keeps vectors alongside structured/semi-structured data

- Works with existing Mongo-style queries

- Simplifies dev stack (one DB for vectors + metadata)

Cons:

- Not optimized for large-scale vector search (slower than OpenSearch or Redis)

- Requires careful tuning of `numCandidates` for accuracy/speed balance

Feature Comparison Table

Feature	OpenSearch	MemoryDB	DocumentDB

387

Latency	Medium (20–100ms)	Ultra-low (<10ms)	Medium-High (50ms+)
Index Type	knn_vector	VECTOR HNSW	vector
Filtering	☑ Yes (hybrid)	✖ Manual only	☑ Basic query filters
Scale	High (horizontal)	Medium (sharding)	Low-Medium
Ideal Use Case	RAG, search, NLP	Realtime cache	Personalized recs
Vector Storage Cost	Storage-efficient	Memory-heavy	Storage-efficient
Integration Simplicity	Moderate	Simple (redis-py)	Simple (boto3, PyMongo)

🧠 Use Case Recommendations

Use Case	Best Option	Why
Real-time chatbot with LLM	**MemoryDB**	Sub-ms speed for chat sessions
RAG assistant with documents	**OpenSearch**	Hybrid semantic + keyword search
User profile similarity	**DocumentDB**	Embed vectors with JSON profiles
Dynamic product recommendations	**OpenSearch / Redis**	Redis if real-time, OpenSearch if hybrid

ML training data deduplication	**DocumentDB or S3**	Slow but simple embedding join
Semantic document index for Bedrock	**OpenSearch**	Easy plugin with Bedrock workflows

- **Reuse embeddings**: Store generated vectors to avoid recomputation (ideal for RAG)

- **Normalize vectors**: Especially when using cosine similarity

- **Avoid sparse vectors**: Dense embeddings perform better in HNSW or Faiss

- **Cache short-term queries**: Use MemoryDB for chatbot sessions or daily top queries

- **Filter pre-vector**: Always filter the candidate pool before running k-NN

🧬 Appendix G: Data Preparation Tips

Making your data AI/ML-ready across structured, semi-structured, and unstructured pipelines

"Garbage in, garbage out" still applies—especially in AI/ML. Whether you're training a model with tabular records or prompting a large language model (LLM) with a document corpus, **data preparation is everything**. This appendix focuses on **feature engineering best practices**, **file format guidance**, and how to structure data depending on whether you're working with **tabular models or LLM-based systems**.

🧠 1. Feature Engineering Best Practices

Feature engineering is where raw data becomes **model intelligence**. Whether you're working with SQL queries or NoSQL documents, these principles apply:

☑ Best Practices:

Strategy	Description
Use domain logic	Engineer features that reflect real-world behavior (e.g., time since last purchase)
Reduce cardinality	Avoid using high-cardinality fields (e.g., UUIDs) unless embedding
Time-aware features	Use time windows (e.g., rolling avg, last 7 days) instead of point-in-time

Categorical encoding	One-hot encoding for small sets; embeddings for large ones
Normalize numerics	Apply min-max or z-score normalization for tree or linear models
Log-transform skewed data	Improves stability in regression tasks
Handle missing values	Use imputation (mean/mode/flag), not just drop rows
Track feature provenance	Know how/when each feature was derived for reproducibility

Example: Aurora SQL Feature Script

```sql
SELECT
    customer_id,
    COUNT(*) AS txn_count_last_30d,
    AVG(txn_amount) AS avg_txn_amt,
    MAX(txn_amount) AS max_txn_amt,
    DATEDIFF(NOW(), MAX(txn_date)) AS
days_since_last_txn
FROM transactions
WHERE txn_date >= DATE_SUB(NOW(), INTERVAL
30 DAY)
GROUP BY customer_id;
```

📁 2. File Format Guidance (For S3, Redshift, SageMaker, Glue)

The right format can reduce storage, speed up processing, and simplify schema evolution.

Format	Best For	Pros	Cons
CSV	Tabular data, small pipelines	Human-readable, simple	Large, slow, no schema
JSON	Semi-structured, hierarchical data	Flexible, nested fields	Verbose, no compression
Parquet	Big data pipelines, Glue, Redshift	Compressed, columnar, schema-aware	Not human-readable
JSONL	LLM training, line-by-line documents	Streaming-friendly, LLM-compatible	Messy if deeply nested
Avro	High-throughput pipelines	Compact, schema evolution built-in	Complex to inspect
Text	LLMs, embedding generation	Raw format for tokenization	No structure at all

> ◆ *Parquet is generally the best default for training tabular models at scale. JSONL is your go-to for LLM fine-tuning or RAG pipelines.*

🤖 3. Structuring Data for LLMs vs. Tabular ML

Element	Tabular ML Model	LLM / Generative AI
Data Type	Rows and columns	Free text, documents, conversations
Preprocessing	Normalization, encoding	Tokenization, context chunking
Feature Source	Numeric/categorical variables	Textual knowledge, metadata
Training Input	Vectors / numerical matrices	Text sequences (prompts + context)
Preferred Format	CSV / Parquet	JSONL / Text / Markdown

Label Format	Discrete class / number	Expected response / next token

LLM Data Preparation Example (JSONL)

```
{"instruction": "Summarize this support
ticket.", "input": "The customer says the
payment gateway failed after an update.",
"output": "The user reports a failed
transaction due to a recent update."}
```

Used for:

- Fine-tuning LLMs via SageMaker JumpStart or Hugging Face transformers

- Creating synthetic support datasets

- Training QA bots

Tabular ML Input Example (CSV)

```
customer_id,txn_count_last_30d,avg_txn_amt
,days_since_last_txn,is_fraud
12345,7,42.85,2,0
54321,14,512.99,0,1
```

Used for:

- Classification/regression models in SageMaker or XGBoost

- Fraud prediction, churn, LTV scoring

⚠ Common Pitfalls to Avoid

Pitfall	Fix
Mixing data from different timeframes	Time-align your features and labels
Using PII in training	Anonymize or tokenize sensitive fields
Training on leakage	Don't use post-event features (e.g., labels in inputs)
Format mismatch in training/inference	Keep consistent preprocessing pipelines via Glue or code
Inconsistent JSONL structure	Use schema validators or data contracts

---

☑ Summary Tips

- Use **Parquet or JSONL** depending on model type (tabular vs LLM)

- Normalize and encode features properly before model ingestion

- Design features with **business meaning + statistical value**

- For LLMs, chunk context wisely and **track input/output tokens**

- Consider **data versioning tools** (e.g., LakeFS, DVC) for auditability

📖 Appendix H: Glossary

Acronyms & cloud-native ML terms used throughout the book, ordered by relevance to core concepts

This glossary helps you decode the most commonly used acronyms and cloud-native terms found across AWS documentation, architecture diagrams, and this book. It's especially useful if you're jumping between services like SageMaker, Aurora, OpenSearch, and vector-enabled workloads.

🐢 Most Frequently Used Terms

Term	Meaning
RAG	Retrieval-Augmented Generation — combines LLMs with external search (e.g., OpenSearch, MemoryDB) to ground responses with factual context
LLM	Large Language Model — foundational model (e.g., Claude, Titan, GPT) trained on massive corpora
ML	Machine Learning — teaching algorithms to learn from data and make predictions
AI	Artificial Intelligence — broader field involving logic, reasoning, generation, and learning
IAM	Identity and Access Management — controls who can do what in your AWS environment
VPC	Virtual Private Cloud — isolated networking environment for your AWS resources
S3	Amazon Simple Storage Service — object storage used in virtually all ML data pipelines
EC2	Elastic Compute Cloud — AWS virtual machines, often used for custom ML environments

CLI	Command Line Interface — used to interact with AWS services via terminal
SDK	Software Development Kit — AWS SDKs (like boto3) let you automate everything from Python or JavaScript

🏦 Database and Data Pipeline Terms

Term	Meaning
Aurora	AWS's high-performance managed relational database (compatible with MySQL/PostgreSQL)
DocumentDB	Managed JSON document database compatible with MongoDB
Neptune	AWS's fully managed graph database service
OpenSearch	AWS's managed search and analytics engine, supports full-text and vector queries
MemoryDB	In-memory database service with Redis compatibility and vector search support
Glue	Serverless ETL and data prep engine in AWS
Redshift	Columnar data warehouse optimized for analytics
Feature Store	Storage for engineered ML features used in training and inference
Change Stream	DocumentDB feature to capture real-time inserts/updates
Activity Stream	Aurora feature for streaming real-time query logs and database activity

⚙ ML Workflow & Infrastructure Acronyms

Term	Meaning

ETL	Extract, Transform, Load — pipeline pattern for preparing and loading data
Zero-ETL	AWS-native integrations that remove the need for manual ETL (e.g., Aurora → Redshift)
ECS	Elastic Container Service — run containerized workloads in AWS
EKS	Elastic Kubernetes Service — run Kubernetes clusters in AWS
Fargate	Serverless compute engine for containers
Lambda	AWS's serverless compute engine triggered by events
Step Functions	AWS's visual workflow service — often used to orchestrate ML pipelines
SageMaker	AWS's flagship ML platform for training, hosting, and deploying models
Bedrock	AWS-managed service to access foundation models (Claude, Titan, etc.)
JumpStart	Prebuilt ML solutions and models in SageMaker

🔐 Security & Compliance Acronyms

Term	Meaning
KMS	Key Management Service — handles encryption keys for secure data access
ACM	AWS Certificate Manager — issues and manages SSL/TLS certs
SCP	Service Control Policy — governs what actions accounts in an AWS Org can take
CloudTrail	Logs all AWS API calls for auditing and compliance
Macie	AWS tool for detecting sensitive data (PII, PHI) in S3 buckets
WAF	Web Application Firewall — protects web apps from common exploits

🔬 AI Modeling Terms

Term	Meaning
Embedding	Vectorized numerical representation of text or other data for ML similarity
Vector Index	Specialized index for fast similarity search on embeddings
k-NN	k-Nearest Neighbors — algorithm for finding the most similar items
HNSW	Hierarchical Navigable Small World — vector search algorithm used in Redis
ANN	Approximate Nearest Neighbors — faster, less exact version of k-NN
LTR	Learning to Rank — model that ranks search results by predicted relevance
NLP	Natural Language Processing — AI techniques for working with human language
Prompt Engineering	Designing inputs to guide LLM behavior

📦 DevOps and Monitoring

Term	Meaning
CloudWatch	Centralized metrics, logs, and alarms service in AWS
X-Ray	Distributed tracing tool for microservices and Lambda
Trusted Advisor	Gives AWS best practice recommendations on cost, security, and performance
Cost Explorer	Helps you analyze and visualize your AWS costs
Pricing Calculator	AWS tool for estimating service costs in advance

🐝 Appendix I: Cost Estimation Templates

3 real-world AI/ML stacks on AWS with service-level breakdowns and optimization strategies

Deploying AI/ML pipelines on AWS can quickly rack up costs—especially when vector search, inference, and multi-region storage are involved. This appendix gives you **3 stack examples** with estimated costs, **per-service breakdowns**, and **real-world optimization tips**.

All costs are **approximate**, based on AWS public pricing (as of early 2025), assuming **us-east-1** region and light-to-medium production workloads.

🎁 Stack 1: RAG-Powered Chatbot (Bedrock + OpenSearch)

Use Case: An AI assistant that answers questions using semantic search over private documents.

🔧 Stack Components:

Service	Description	Est. Monthly Cost
Amazon Bedrock	1M token generation (Claude v2)	$100–150
OpenSearch	3-node cluster w/ vector k-NN	$300–500
S3	Document store (10GB)	<$5
Lambda	Vector queries + orchestration	$15–30
MemoryDB (optional)	Cache recent chat history	$60–100

CloudWatch Logs	Monitoring + inference tracing	$5–10
Total		**$500–800**

💡 Optimization Tips:

- Use **Bedrock Streaming APIs** to pay per output token, not compute time

- Compress and chunk documents before vectorizing

- Store embeddings in **OpenSearch Cold Tier** for infrequent docs

- Use **multi-tenant chat context** to share memory across users

---

🖼 Stack 2: Fraud Detection Pipeline (Aurora → SageMaker)

Use Case: Real-time transaction monitoring using ML inference via SageMaker.

🔧 Stack Components:

Service	Description	Est. Monthly Cost
Aurora PostgreSQL	db.r6g.large (primary + replica)	$300–400
SageMaker Endpoint	Real-time XGBoost inference (ml.m5.large)	$80–150
Lambda	Stream from Aurora → ML call	$20–40
Kinesis Data Stream	Capture Aurora Activity Streams	$50–80

401

S3	Store transaction logs	<$10
CloudTrail + Logs	Access logging	$5–15
Total		**$500–700**

💡 Optimization Tips:

- Switch to **Aurora Serverless v2** for bursty traffic patterns

- Enable **multi-model endpoints** in SageMaker to consolidate costs

- Pre-aggregate low-risk transactions in Lambda (skip ML call)

- Stream transaction batches and run **batch transform** jobs for low-priority use cases

---

🧬 Stack 3: Graph-Based ML Feature Extraction (Neptune → SageMaker)

Use Case: Build user community features from graph data for recommendation models.

🔧 Stack Components:

Service	Description	Est. Monthly Cost
Neptune	db.r5.xlarge + 1 replica	$500–600
SageMaker Notebook	Model prototyping (ml.t3.medium)	$25–50
Glue Job	Extract features from graph	$40–60

S3	Store feature tables & raw graph data	$10–20
IAM Roles + Logs	Audit and access logs	$5–10
Total		**$600–800**

💡 Optimization Tips:

- Export graph data to **CSV/Parquet via Neptune Export** before feature engineering

- Use **SageMaker Processing Jobs** for one-time batch transforms

- Turn off dev endpoints when not in use

- Apply **gremlin query optimization** to reduce traversal depth and IOPS

📊 Summary Table

Stack	Total Est. Cost	Key Cost Drivers	Primary Optimization Areas
RAG Chatbot (Bedrock + OpenSearch)	$500–800	OpenSearch cluster, Bedrock	Token limits, caching, cold tier
Fraud Detection (Aurora + SageMaker)	$500–700	Aurora + real-time endpoints	Serverless Aurora, multi-model usage
Graph ML (Neptune + SageMaker)	$600–800	Neptune, Glue jobs	Feature preloading, query tuning

🛠️ Tools to Estimate Your Own Stack

- AWS Pricing Calculator

- `costexplorer:GetCostAndUsage` **for building** dashboards

- CloudWatch → Contributor Insights for noisy service alerts

- **AWS Budgets** with alert thresholds on service-specific spend

---

📖 **Appendix J:** Useful Links and Further Reading

A curated set of links to official AWS documentation, learning paths, open-source tools, and relevant case studies mentioned throughout this book.

Whether you're continuing your journey into AI/ML on AWS, exploring vector search in production, or diving deeper into database architectures, the resources below will keep you moving forward.

🌐 Official AWS Documentation

Topic	Link
Amazon Aurora	https://docs.aws.amazon.com/AmazonRDS/latest/AuroraUserGuide/
Amazon DocumentDB	https://docs.aws.amazon.com/documentdb/latest/developerguide/
Amazon Neptune	https://docs.aws.amazon.com/neptune/latest/userguide/
Amazon MemoryDB	https://docs.aws.amazon.com/memorydb/latest/devguide/
Amazon OpenSearch Service	https://docs.aws.amazon.com/opensearch-service/latest/developerguide/
Amazon SageMaker	https://docs.aws.amazon.com/sagemaker/latest/dg/
Amazon Bedrock	https://docs.aws.amazon.com/bedrock/latest/userguide/

AWS IAM	https://docs.aws.amazon.com/IAM/latest/UserGuide/
Amazon S3	https://docs.aws.amazon.com/AmazonS3/latest/userguide/
AWS Lambda	https://docs.aws.amazon.com/lambda/latest/dg/
AWS Glue	https://docs.aws.amazon.com/glue/latest/dg/

📊 AI/ML on AWS — Learning Paths

Resource Type	Link
ML on AWS Ramp-Up Guide	https://aws.amazon.com/training/learning-paths/machine-learning/
Free AWS ML Courses (via Skill Builder)	https://explore.skillbuilder.aws/learn/course/13471/ml-building-blocks
AWS GenAI Learning Plan	https://explore.skillbuilder.aws/learn/public/learning_plan/view/137/generative-ai-learning-plan
AWS SageMaker Studio Lab	https://studiolab.sagemaker.aws/

🔍 Vector Search & RAG

Tool / Guide	Link
Vector Search in OpenSearch	https://docs.aws.amazon.com/opensearch-service/latest/developerguide/vector-search.html
Vector Search in MemoryDB	https://docs.aws.amazon.com/memorydb/latest/devguide/vector-search.html
DocumentDB Vector Indexing	https://docs.aws.amazon.com/documentdb/latest/developerguide/vector-search.html
Retrieval-Augmented Generation on AWS	https://aws.amazon.com/blogs/machine-learning/how-to-build-rag-pipelines-using-amazon-bedrock-and-vector-databases/

406

Architecture & Security References

Topic	Link
AWS Well-Architected Framework	https://docs.aws.amazon.com/wellarchitected/latest/framework/
AWS Architecture Center	https://aws.amazon.com/architecture/
Security Best Practices	https://docs.aws.amazon.com/securityhub/latest/userguide/securityhub-standards-fsbp.html
IAM Policy Reference	https://docs.aws.amazon.com/IAM/latest/UserGuide/reference_policies_elements.html

Case Studies & Real-World Architectures

Company/Use Case	Link
Netflix + Graph Data (Neptune)	https://aws.amazon.com/blogs/database/how-netflix-uses-amazon-neptune-to-power-its-entertainment-graph/
Duolingo + Redis Vector	https://redis.com/blog/duolingo-redis-vector-search/
Intuit + Aurora Scaling	https://aws.amazon.com/solutions/case-studies/intuit-aurora-case-study/
Redfin + OpenSearch	https://aws.amazon.com/opensearch-service/customers/
FINRA + Real-Time Analytics	https://aws.amazon.com/blogs/big-data/finra-analytics-on-aws/

Open-Source Tools Mentioned

Tool	Link
FAISS (Facebook AI Similarity Search)	https://github.com/facebookresearch/faiss
LangChain for AWS	https://docs.langchain.com/integrations/providers/aws/
Pinecone (alt. vector db)	https://docs.pinecone.io/docs/aws-integration

| Redis + RediSearch | https://oss.redis.com/redisearch/ |
| Hugging Face Transformers | https://huggingface.co/docs/transformers/index |

🔧 Cost Estimation & Budgeting

Tool / Guide	Link
AWS Pricing Calculator	https://calculator.aws.amazon.com/
AWS Budgets	https://docs.aws.amazon.com/cost-management/latest/userguide/budgets-managing-costs.html
AWS Free Tier	https://aws.amazon.com/free/

📖 Appendix K: Explore More from the Author

Expand your AWS knowledge with these in-depth technical guides by Souren Stepanyan

Whether you're building microservices, securing access policies, or deploying scalable data pipelines, each book in this series is written to help you **master specific AWS services** with real-world patterns, SDK examples, and architecture insights.

📚 Available Books in the Series

Title	Description
Mastering AWS Lambda	Deep dive into serverless functions, event-driven design, integration with API Gateway, and more
Mastering Amazon S3	Covers S3 internals, lifecycle management, versioning, performance tuning, and secure access
Mastering AWS DynamoDB	Learn how to model, query, and scale NoSQL apps with DynamoDB best practices
Mastering AWS IAM	Practical guide to building secure, least-privilege access policies and multi-account strategies
Mastering Amazon OpenSearch	Architecting powerful search, analytics, and vector workloads with OpenSearch on AWS
Mastering Amazon MemoryDB	High-performance Redis and vector search for real-time AI/ML apps and caching
Mastering Amazon DocumentDB	Harness JSON, vector search, and change streams for flexible ML-ready NoSQL solutions
Mastering Amazon Aurora *(upcoming)*	Architecture, performance, and real-world relational patterns for AI/ML and serverless workloads

📦 Bundle Themes

🎯 Serverless + Event-Driven

- AWS Lambda

- S3 (event notifications)

- DynamoDB streams

🔒 Security & Access Control

- AWS IAM

- Fine-grained OpenSearch and DocumentDB access

- Lambda + IAM boundaries

📊 AI/ML-Focused

- OpenSearch vector search

- DocumentDB embeddings + change streams

- MemoryDB semantic caching

- Aurora ML SQL inference

- This book: *AWS Databases for AI/ML*

🌐 Where to Get Them

- 📖 **Amazon KDP**: Author Page
  https://www.amazon.com/author/sourenstepanyan

- 🌸 **Medium Blog**: programming.am
  https://programming.am

- ⚪ **Official Website**: sourenstepanyan.com
  https://sourenstepanyan.com

- 🔺 **Project Hub (Coming Soon)**: awsblueprints.dev
  https://awsblueprints.dev

✉ Stay in the Loop

Sign up at awsblueprints.dev/newsletter (placeholder) to:

- Get early access to upcoming books

- Receive architecture templates and real-world guides

- Join community Q&A sessions

📚 Discover More Books by the Author

Take your AWS skills further with Souren Stepanyan's growing collection of deep-dive technical books. Each title is focused, practical, and packed with real-world strategies.

◇ Mastering AWS Lambda

Design scalable, event-driven applications with Lambda, API Gateway, and Step Functions. Learn how to integrate with other AWS services, secure your functions, and monitor performance.

https://www.amazon.com/dp/B0DJ6CMJY5

◇ Mastering Amazon S3

Beyond simple storage: master lifecycle policies, cross-region replication, static website hosting, and advanced security patterns for Amazon S3.

https://www.amazon.com/dp/B0DJ6HJJBQ

◇ Mastering AWS DynamoDB

Model, query, and scale NoSQL workloads with confidence. Includes real-world schema designs, indexing patterns, and performance tuning techniques.

https://www.amazon.com/dp/B0DQ2C822D

◇ Mastering AWS IAM

Your complete guide to building secure, least-privilege access control for users, services, and resources in AWS. Includes hands-on policy examples and role-based architectures.

https://www.amazon.com/dp/B0DQ1G8ZTK

◇ Mastering Amazon OpenSearch

Build blazing-fast search and analytics systems with full-text indexing, vector search, and real-time anomaly detection. Ideal for ML and GenAI workloads.

https://www.amazon.com/dp/B0F2GHWS3Y

◇ Mastering Amazon MemoryDB

Build ultra-low-latency AI/ML pipelines using Redis-compatible MemoryDB with vector search support. Ideal for real-time caching, personalization, and RAG pipelines.

https://www.amazon.com/dp/B0CZVD6SVY

◇ Mastering Amazon DocumentDB

Leverage MongoDB-compatible DocumentDB for vector search, change streams, and schema-aware ML pipelines.

https://www.amazon.com/dp/B0F2SGB9K3

◇ Mastering Amazon Aurora

Architect high-performance, SQL-based data layers for AI/ML pipelines using Aurora PostgreSQL and MySQL. Includes Aurora ML, global DB, and

Zero-ETL strategies.

https://www.amazon.com/dp/B0F31L5V27

◇ Mastering Amazon Neptune Analytics

Mastering Amazon Neptune Analytics

Unlock the power of graph-based AI and machine learning with real-time pathfinding, community detection, vector similarity, and knowledge graph enrichment using Amazon Neptune.

https://www.amazon.com/dp/B0F2MYWWFJ

www.ingramcontent.com/pod-product-compliance
Lightning Source LLC
Chambersburg PA
CBHW070931050326
40689CB00014B/3160